ARBITRARY BORDERS

Political Boundaries in World History

The Division of the Middle East
The Treaty of Sèvres

Northern Ireland and England
The Troubles

The Great Wall of China

The Green Line
The Division of Palestine

The Iron Curtain
The Cold War in Europe

The Mason–Dixon Line

Vietnam: The 17th Parallel

**Korea: The 38th Parallel and
the Demilitarized Zone**

The U.S.–Mexico Border
The Treaty of Guadalupe Hidalgo

**The Czech Republic:
The Velvet Revolution**

Louisiana Territory

**South Africa:
A State of Apartheid**

The Partition of British India

**London: From the Walled City
to New Towns**

**A South American Frontier:
The Tri-Border Region**

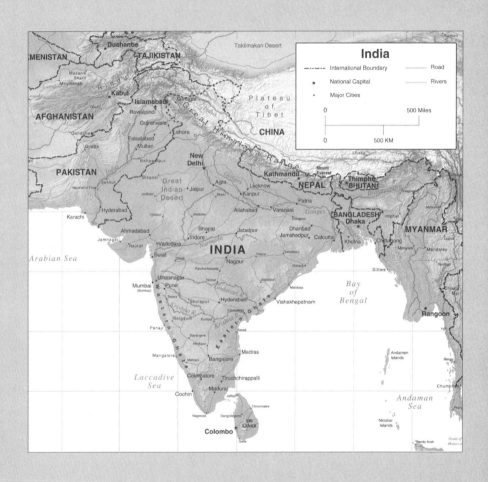

The Partition
of British India

Jeff Hay

San Diego State University

Foreword by
Senator George J. Mitchell

Introduction by
James I. Matray
California State University, Chico

CHELSEA HOUSE
P U B L I S H E R S

An imprint of Infobase Publishing

FRONTIS The border between India and Pakistan has been disputed since 1947, when Great Britain partitioned British colonial India to create a Hindu and a Muslim state. The border, pictured on this map, was created by London lawyer Cyril Radcliffe and a committee of eight Indian judges.

The Partition of British India

Chelsea House
An imprint of Infobase Publishing
132 West 31st Street
New York NY 10001

Library of Congress Cataloging-in-Publication Data

Hay, Jeff.
  The partition of British India / Jeff Hay.
     p. cm. — (Arbitrary borders)
  Includes bibliographical references and index.
  ISBN 0-7910-8647-X
  1. India—History—Partition, 1947. I. Title. II. Series.
  DS480.842.H42 2006
  954.03'59—dc22   2005031772

Chelsea House books are available at special discounts when purchased in bulk quantities for businesses, associations, institutions, or sales promotions. Please call our Special Sales Department in New York at (212) 967–8800 or (800) 322–8755.

You can find Chelsea House on the World Wide Web at
http://www.chelseahouse.com

Text design by Takeshi Takahashi
Cover design by Keith Trego

Printed in the United States of America

Bang EJB 10 9 8 7 6 5 4 3 2 1

This book is printed on acid-free paper.

All links and web addresses were checked and verified to be correct at the time of publication. Because of the dynamic nature of the web, some addresses and links may have changed since publication and may no longer be valid.

Contents

Foreword

Senator George J. Mitchell

I spent years working for peace in Northern Ireland and in the Middle East. I also made many visits to the Balkans during the long and violent conflict there.

Each of the three areas is unique; so is each conflict. But there are also some similarities: in each, there are differences over religion, national identity, and territory.

Deep religious differences that lead to murderous hostility are common in human history. Competing aspirations involving national identity are more recent occurrences, but often have been just as deadly.

Territorial disputes—two or more people claiming the same land—are as old as humankind. Almost without exception, such disputes have been a factor in recent conflicts. It is impossible to calculate the extent to which the demand for land—as opposed to religion, national identity, or other factors—figures in the motivation of people caught up in conflict. In my experience it is a substantial factor that has played a role in each of the three conflicts mentioned above.

In Northern Ireland and the Middle East, the location of the border was a major factor in igniting and sustaining the conflict. And it is memorialized in a dramatic and visible way: through the construction of large walls whose purpose is to physically separate the two communities.

In Belfast, the capital and largest city in Northern Ireland, the so-called "Peace Line" cuts through the heart of the city, right across urban streets. Up to thirty feet high in places, topped with barbed wire in others, it is an ugly reminder of the duration and intensity of the conflict.

In the Middle East, as I write these words, the government of Israel has embarked on a huge and controversial effort to construct a security fence roughly along the line that separates Israel from the West Bank.

Having served a tour of duty with the U.S. Army in Berlin, which was once the site of the best known of modern walls, I am skeptical of their long-term value, although they often serve short-term needs. But it cannot be said that such structures represent a new idea. Ancient China built the Great Wall to deter nomadic Mongol tribes from attacking its population.

In much the same way, other early societies established boundaries and fortified them militarily to achieve the goal of self-protection. Borders always have separated people. Indeed, that is their purpose.

This series of books examines the important and timely issue of the significance of arbitrary borders in history. Each volume focuses attention on a territorial division, but the analytical approach is more comprehensive. These studies describe arbitrary borders as places where people interact differently from the way they would if the boundary did not exist. This pattern is especially pronounced where there is no geographic reason for the boundary and no history recognizing its legitimacy. Even though many borders have been defined without legal precision, governments frequently have provided vigorous monitoring and military defense for them.

This series will show how the migration of people and exchange of goods almost always work to undermine the separation that borders seek to maintain. The continuing evolution of a European community provides a contemporary example illustrating this point, most obviously with the adoption of a single currency. Moreover, even former Soviet bloc nations have eliminated barriers to economic and political integration.

Globalization has emerged as one of the most powerful forces in international affairs during the twenty-first century. Not only have markets for the exchange of goods and services become genuinely worldwide, but instant communication and sharing of information have shattered old barriers separating people. Some scholars even argue that globalization has made the entire concept of a territorial nation-state irrelevant. Although the assertion is certainly premature and probably wrong, it highlights the importance of recognizing how borders often have reflected and affirmed the cultural, ethnic, or linguistic perimeters that define a people or a country.

Since the Cold War ended, competition over resources or a variety of interests threaten boundaries more than ever, resulting in contentious interaction, conflict, adaptation, and intermixture. How people define their borders is also a factor in determining how events develop in the surrounding region. This series will provide detailed descriptions of selected arbitrary borders in history with the objective of providing insights on how artificial boundaries separating people will influence international affairs during the next century.

Senator George J. Mitchell
September 2005

Introduction

James I. Matray
California State University, Chico

Throughout history, borders have separated people. Scholars have devoted considerable attention to assessing the significance and impact of territorial boundaries on the course of human history, explaining how they often have been sources of controversy and conflict. In the modern age, the rise of nation-states in Europe created the need for governments to negotiate treaties to confirm boundary lines that periodically changed as a consequence of wars and revolutions. European expansion in the nineteenth century imposed new borders on Africa and Asia. Many native peoples viewed these boundaries as arbitrary and, after independence, continued to contest their legitimacy. At the end of both world wars in the twentieth century, world leaders drew artificial and impermanent lines separating assorted people around the globe. Borders certainly are among the most important factors that have influenced the development of world affairs.

Chelsea House Publishers decided to publish a collection of books looking at arbitrary borders in history in response to the revival of the nuclear crisis in North Korea in October 2002. Recent tensions on the Korean peninsula are a direct consequence of Korea's partition at the 38th parallel at the end of World War II. Other nations in human history have suffered because of similar artificial divisions that have been the result of either international or domestic factors and often a combination of both. In the case of Korea, the United States and the Soviet Union decided in August 1945 to divide the country into two zones of military occupation ostensibly to facilitate the surrender of Japanese forces. However, a political contest was then underway inside Korea to determine the future of the nation after forty years of Japanese colonial rule. The Cold War then created two Koreas with sharply contrasting political, social, and economic systems that symbolized an ideological split among the Korean people. Borders separate people, but rarely prevent their economic, political, social, and cultural interaction. But in Korea, an artificial border has existed since 1945 as a nearly impenetrable barrier precluding meaningful contact between two portions of the same population. Ultimately, two authentic Koreas emerged, exposing how an arbitrary boundary can create circumstances resulting even in the permanent division of a homogeneous people in a historically united land.

Korea's experience in dealing with artificial division may well be unique, but it is not without historical parallels. The first group of books in this series on arbitrary boundaries provided description and analysis of the division of the Middle East after World War I, the Iron Curtain in Central Europe during the Cold War, the United States-Mexico Border, the 17th parallel in Vietnam, and the Mason-Dixon Line. Three authors in a second set of studies addressed the Great Wall in China, the Green Line in Israel, and the 38th parallel and demilitarized zone in Korea. Four other volumes described how discord over artificial borders in the Louisiana Territory, Northern Ireland, Czechoslovakia, and South Africa provide insights about fundamental disputes focusing on sovereignty, religion, and ethnicity. Six books now complete the series. Three authors explore the role of arbitrary boundaries in shaping the history of the city of London, the partition of British India, and the Tri-Border Region in Latin America. Finally, there are studies examining Britain's dispute with Spain over Gibraltar, Modern China, and the splintering of Yugoslavia after the end of the Cold War.

Admittedly, there are many significant differences between these boundaries, but these books will strive to cover as many common themes as possible. In so doing, each will help readers conceptualize how complex factors such as colonialism, culture, and economics determine the nature of contact between people along these borders. Although globalization has emerged as a powerful force working against the creation and maintenance of lines separating people, boundaries likely will endure as factors having a persistent influence on world events. This series of books will provide insights about the impact of arbitrary borders on human history and how such borders continue to shape the modern world.

James I. Matray
Chico, California
September 2005

1

Kashmir:
A Disputed
Province

Kashmir—the Mughal Emperor Jehangir, who reigned over most of India from 1605 to 1627, loved it there. He considered this northern region of wooded mountains, fragrant valleys, streams, and lakes, with its views of the high Karakoram Mountains to the north, the nearest place possible to an earthly paradise. He once said that Kashmir was "a page that the painter of destiny had drawn with the pencil of creation."[1] Jehangir built the Shalimar Gardens there, in the renowned valley, or "vale" of Kashmir and dedicated the site to his wife Nur Jahan, whose name means the "light of the world." Containing four pavilions called "abodes of love," as well as rich and varied lines of plants, trees, flowers, and fountains, Nur Jahan's Shalimar is one of many Kashmiri pleasure gardens constructed by Jehangir and other Mughal emperors.

The British, who followed the Mughals as India's rulers and constructed a new set of arbitrary geographical, cultural, and economic boundaries in the extremely diverse land, also loved Kashmir. They transformed it into a top spot for holidays and other escapes from the hot plains to the south. Their attachment to it was somewhat less romantic than that of the Mughals, but nevertheless they were drawn to the landscape, to the gardens, and to life on houseboats in flower-strewn Dal Lake in the Kashmiri capital city of Srinigar. In their attempt to turn the region into a British-style paradise, they built golf courses, set up hunting lodges in the woods, and stocked mountain streams with Scottish trout.

In 1947, when India became independent, Kashmir was one of India's many princely states. These were half-independent kingdoms that for the most part had been left alone by the British. The ruler of Kashmir, Maharajah Hari Singh, was a Hindu. Most of the people living in Kashmir, however, were Muslims. As part of the independence agreements reached between British and Indian officials, princely states like Kashmir were forced to accede to one or the other new nations into which India would be partitioned, according to new arbitrary borderlines: mostly Hindu India or Muslim Pakistan. Most of the

During the partition process, Hari Singh, the last maharaja of Kashmir and a Hindu, decided to cede the predominately Muslim state to India, rather than Pakistan. Over the subsequent decades, India and Pakistan have fought three wars over the disputed territory and today it remains a point of contention. Singh is pictured here (center) in April 1944, while visiting Great Britain.

princes acceded quickly, but Hari Singh could not make up his mind, and, when India's and Pakistan's independence celebrations took place in mid-August, 1947, the status of Kashmir was still unclear. The maharaja apparently hoped that, somehow, his state could remain independent of either country.

On October 21, 1947, an army of 5,000 entered Kashmir. They were Muslim Pathan tribesmen, members of a vast network of tribal groups who traditionally cared little about border arrangements in northwestern India and neighboring Afghanistan. The motives for this invasion were unclear. Some claim that it was approved by Pakistan's government. Others say that it was an independent act on the part of Pathans seeking redress for communal difficulties in Jammu, a Hindu-dominated sister state to Kashmir. Regardless, Hari Singh's own Hindu officers deserted him, and his meager army joined the Pathans as they made their way toward Srinigar. If they took the city, it was probable that Hari Singh would be forced to cede his state to Pakistan.

In many ways, it made sense for Kashmir to join Pakistan. Not only was the population mostly Muslim, but geography favored the union. Land routes between the two were open year-round, whereas the only land connection between Kashmir and India would often be closed in winter because of the snows. In addition, the Indus River, which traverses all of Pakistan and waters much of it, originates in southwestern Tibet and flows into Kashmir. Many Hindu leaders, in fact, assumed that Kashmir would become Pakistani. One of them, Vallabhbhai Patel, slyly noted that "it would not be taken amiss by India" if Kashmir joined Pakistan.[2] India's Prime Minister, Jawaharlal Nehru, meanwhile, had a sentimental attachment to the state: He had been born there, and his ancestors were Kashmiri Brahmins, members of one of Hinduism's highest castes.

Upon hearing of the Pathan invasion, British Field Marshal Lord Auchinleck, who had been asked to stay on by the new Indian government, proposed sending troops to Srinigar to protect Britishers caught up in the turmoil. India's governor-general Lord Louis Mountbatten, the top British official in the new state, refused. He was hesitant to approve any rash moves that might commit Britain to a war between what were now two sovereign nations. Tens of thousands had already died in communal violence as the arbitrary borders that now separated India and Pakistan became known.

Hari Singh was in a panic, fearful now that he might not only lose his throne but his life. On October 26, he agreed to cede Kashmir not to Pakistan, but to India, and he formally asked India for military help to oust the Pathans. Mountbatten agreed, but only on the condition that in the near future a vote be held; he wanted Kashmir's people to decide themselves whether they were to be Indian or Pakistani. The Indian government agreed to the condition and dispatched the First Sikh Batallion to Srinigar by air to defend the city. The Sikhs were followed by aircraft that would evacuate remaining Britishers, as well as other refugees, from what was now a war zone.

Others had already begun their escape by bus. British citizens were lucky; they could go to either India or Pakistan relatively easily and safely, since on all sides of the borders, even rioters avoided harming the British. Hindus and Muslims were not so fortunate. A British woman, Feh Williams, escaped Srinigar by bus on October 24. Her first destination was the Pakistani city of Rawalpindi, and she took with her a Hindu servant. They made it to Rawalpindi relatively easily, but Williams wanted to go on to Delhi to rejoin her husband, an officer on Auchinleck's staff. She refused to leave behind her Hindu servant in a Pakistan where Hindus were unwelcome, however. Few trains were running between India and Pakistan at that time, and in any case neither the rails nor the roads could be considered safe. Williams's servant, for her part, refused to disguise herself in order to avoid being identified as a Hindu. The two finally reached Delhi by air in mid-November, but only after Auchinleck himself intervened.[3]

By that time, there were tens of thousands of Indian troops in Kashmir, and 25,000 more Pathan tribesmen had joined those of the earlier invasion. The fighting continued haltingly until an uneasy truce was reached near the end of the year. The Pathans occupied a part of western Kashmir, where they first established a free state called Azad Kashmir, or "Free Kashmir," which they then ceded to Pakistan. On the other side of the lines, Hari Singh abdicated his throne to his more pliable son Karan Singh, who never challenged the Indian claim to the rest of Kashmir, including Srinigar and the renowned vale. From that point on, the Indian government cited Hari Singh's accession agreement as the fact that gave India legal right to Kashmir.

Just like India itself, Kashmir had been partitioned, although this time by direct invasion and conflict rather than through legal means. This state of affairs prevented any vote from ever taking place among the population as a whole. Indian Prime Minister Nehru demanded that before any vote take place, the Pathans withdraw from "Free Kashmir." His Pakistani counterpart, Muhammad Ali Jinnah, demanded that both the Pathans and Indian forces elsewhere leave Kashmir at the same time. Neither backed down. The conflict was finally settled by a cease-fire negotiated by the United Nations that took effect on January 1, 1949. Even though the guns had stopped firing, temporarily, the underlying issues lay unresolved, and Mountbatten's vote never took place. Kashmir, the earthly paradise of the Mughals, is still partitioned, and it was the focus of a second war between India and Pakistan in 1965, as well as of frequent threats of force on both sides in the subsequent years. Since both nations are now official nuclear powers, Kashmir is one of the world's flash-points and one of the most unfortunate legacies of the arbitrary boundaries that divided the Indian subcontinent in 1947.

2

A Diverse Land
of Changing
Borders

India has always been a land of shifting borders, cultural as well as geographical. One of the world's most diverse areas, India has served as the birthplace of several major religions and remains the home of others. Its people speak a wide variety of languages. North India's major languages are related to Latin and Greek and therefore modern English, whereas those of the south are completely different. Further, the subcontinent has attracted visitors and invaders for many centuries. Some came in numbers large enough to alter the course of Indian civilization. Others, often merchants or pilgrims, settled there and were absorbed into the diversity of Indian life. This diversity has often meant that, in India, borders and political arrangements have been mostly temporary.

India's diversity is reflected in its geography. It is a vast area of a million and a half square miles and is today the home of more than 1.2 billion people, if one adds together the population of the modern nations of India, Pakistan, and Bangladesh, which make up much of the historical Indian zone of civilization. In the north, the subcontinent is isolated from China and central Asia by vast mountain ranges, notably the Himalayas. Called by some the "world's ceiling," the Himalayas are the highest mountains on Earth, and they are difficult to traverse. They have also protected India from the climatic influence of the Arctic regions, ensuring that, outside the mountains, the weather is hot rather than temperate. The main entryway into India from the north is the Khyber Pass, which now connects Pakistan and Afghanistan. The pass has been the common route used by invaders.

Several great rivers or river systems start in these mountain ranges. One, the Indus, also now mostly in Pakistan, has given the region its name. Five other rivers—the Jhelum, Beas, Chenab, Ravi, and Sutlej—feed into the Indus before it empties into the Arabian Sea, and they have helped make northwestern India, especially the Punjab, the region's richest agricultural area. Two other great rivers water much of the rest of northern India: the Ganges (Ganga), with its main sister river, the Jamuna, and

The main entryway into India from the north is the Khyber Pass, which today connects Afghanistan and Pakistan. In 1879, the British built the first road through the pass, which, throughout history, has been both a major trade and invasion route to India.

the Brahmaputra. Both empty into the Bay of Bengal, and both have great religious significance for Hindus.

The Himalayan foothills end abruptly in the North Indian plains, which has served as the heartland of Indian civilization for more than 3,000 years. The plains are the site of such great cities as Lahore, Delhi, and Allahabad. Another, Benares (Varanasi), on the Ganges, is thought by many to be the oldest continually inhabited city on Earth, dating back to at least 1000 B.C. Benares is also the holiest city in India for Hindus. Aside from some desert areas to the west, the rivers that water the area, in combination with India's weather pattern of heavy summer monsoon rains followed by a winter cool season and a spring-time hot season, have ensured that the plains are reasonably rich in agricultural production. To the east, where the Ganges splits into numerous and often shifting channels before entering the sea, is Bengal, another area rich in agriculture.

The Vindhya and Satpura Mountains and another great river, the Narmada, separate the North Indian plains from the Deccan Plateau, in India's center. The region traditionally has been a buffer between the fairly different civilizations in India's north and south and has often prevented the south from being conquered by aggressive North Indian kingdoms. In turn, the south is divided by two coastal mountain ranges running on a north-south axis: the Western and Eastern Ghats. Between them is another high plateau. Particularly along the coasts, the south is full of tropical rain forests, making it very different from the alluvial (silt-deposit) plains of the north.

The inhabitants of the south have had frequent contact and interchange with groups outside of India. In the west, for centuries local leaders maintained trade contacts with East Africa and Arabia, and people seeking freedom from religious oppression; even early Jews and Christians, found homes there. The east coast had frequent contact with the island of Sri Lanka, as well as with Burma and other areas of Southeast Asia.

Indian civilization began about 5,000 years ago in the northwestern part of the subcontinent. Then, a major urban civilization arose; it is today known variously as Harappa (after one of its important cities) and the Indus Valley civilization, because it was watered by the regions' rivers. Its writing system has yet to be fully deciphered by archaeologists, so relatively little is known about this ancient civilization. It *is* known, however, that the Harappans were sophisticated city-builders and that they traded with the civilizations of Mesopotamia (Iraq) and Egypt to the west. The Harappan religion is also thought to have worshipped early versions of some of the Hindu gods, lending support to those who claim that Hinduism is both the oldest continuous religion on Earth and is the religion most native to India.

During the centuries of 2000 to 1500 B.C., the Harappan

civilization faded, probably because of deforestation and the exhaustion of the nutrients in the soil from overfarming. Its cities were abandoned, and survivors migrated eastward into the Ganges Delta and to southern India, although they retreated to a lifestyle of small-scale agriculture and villages rather than cities and trade. These peoples are known as Dravidians, and linguistic evidence suggests that their descendants may still predominate in southern India.[4]

After 1500 B.C., India faced its first major wave of invaders and migrants. These were the so-called Indo-Aryans, branches of a larger tribe of Indo-Europeans who settled in Persia (Iran) and throughout Europe, as well as India. Originating probably in southern Russia and the Ukraine, the Indo-Europeans were creative agriculturalists who were likely the first people to domesticate horses and use war chariots in battle. Over several centuries, successive groups of Indo-Aryan migrants established settlements in northern India, and they intermarried with the local people. This genetic mixing was accompanied by cultural interchange in the first major example of Indians crossing arbitrary borders, and it produced the Aryan-Dravidian synthesis that shaped early Indian civilization. The products of this synthesis included Hinduism, shaped by such texts as the Vedas and Upanishads, which include teachings and hymns, and the great epic poems the Mahabharata and Ramayana. These were originally transmitted orally from teacher to student in Sanskrit, Hinduism's sacred, Indo-Aryan language, but were eventually written down, probably between 500 B.C. and A.D. 500.

The settlement of Indo-Aryans in northern India, and their integration with the peoples already there, was rarely peaceful. Much of the Mahabharata, in fact, tells the stories of wars between rival Aryan clans, whereas the Vedas refer frequently to trouble between Aryans and Dravidians. Most of the first true states that emerged from these centuries of warfare, between 1000 and 500 B.C., were the descendants of Aryan tribal groupings led by chieftains known as *rajas*. The pattern of small, local kingdoms remained in place in India for centuries and, even today, the descendants of the rajas who lost their power and states after Indian independence in 1947 enjoy a great deal of prestige.

A major aspect of the Aryan-Dravidian synthesis was the evolution of the caste system, a basic feature of India's social order and of Hinduism. The caste system created divisions among social groups that, in time, hardened into borders that could rarely be crossed. Early Indian society was divided into four main castes based on jobs: In descending order, they were the priestly caste, or *brahmins*; the warrior caste, or *kshatriya*; the productive caste, or *vaisya*; and the laboring caste, or *shudra*. Over the centuries, and as Indian society grew more sophisticated, hundreds of subcastes based on new professions were added to the system. The system may have come about as a sort of racial segregation, with the lighter-skinned and more powerful Indo-Aryans reserving the higher castes for themselves while relegating the darker-skinned Dravidians to the laboring caste or to the truly outcast group known as "untouchables" (today, *dalits*), who performed the dirtiest jobs.

Hindus believe that people are born into their caste and can never leave it. They must marry within their caste and, generally, work at the jobs held by their ancestors. Only after death, and if one performs one's earthly duties, or dharma, properly, can one hope to be reborn at a higher level. The persistence of the caste system has made the Indian social order extremely conservative, and the system is so pervasive that aspects of it, such as the need to marry and live among one's community, were adopted by other groups such as Indian Christians and, later, Muslims. Alternatively, some low-caste Hindus and untouchables adopted these other religions and therefore became free from some caste restrictions.

India's political pattern of division into hundreds of small kingdoms, one example of often-shifting boundaries, has been broken on several occasions, when powerful kings were able to assemble larger empires by establishing dominance over competing or less powerful rajas. The first "unification" of India took place under the Mauryan Dynasty of 326 to 184 B.C., which controlled the kingdom of Magadha in the Ganges plain. Mauryan kings such as Chandragupta, who as a young man reportedly met the Greek conqueror Alexander the Great at the Beas River, in modern Pakistan (the extent of Alexander's conquests), and Ashoka, who converted to Buddhism and helped turn this offshoot of Hinduism into a major faith, controlled much of the subcontinent either directly or through client states. After another several centuries of political disunity, another unification took place under the Gupta kings, also based in Magadha, from A.D. 320 to 550. Like the Mauryans, however, the Guptas never fully controlled the south. They were ousted by a new wave of invaders, Central Asian warriors known as the White Huns. It was to be nearly 1,000 years before most of India was again unified under a single regime.

Islam, born in seventh-century Arabia, arrived in India soon after the Guptas fell. It was carried by merchants, traveling religious teachers, and migrants from the Turkish-speaking world. As others had done before them, Muslim merchants, especially, settled in India's coastal ports and married local women. Thanks to their jobs, they also maintained contact with centers of Islamic civilization elsewhere.

These settlers were followed by Islamic conquerors. The first wave, in the early eleventh century, was led by the Mahmud of Ghazni, a Turkish-speaking warlord from Afghanistan. Mahmud was more interested in plunder than in conquest, however. His successors, following the common route through the Khyber Pass, conquered many of the kingdoms of the North Indian plains and established an imperial capital at Delhi. The "Delhi Sultans" ruled over much of North India until 1526, but their power was weak because they relied on the uneasy support of Hindu kings to maintain order and pay revenue. More powerful states emerged in the Deccan Plateau and the south: first the Chola kingdom (850–1267) and then Vijayanagar (1336–1565). Both were primarily Hindu kingdoms, which exerted their main influence, aside from in the south itself, in Sri Lanka and

Southeast Asia. There was a strong Muslim presence in each area, but it was mostly mercantile rather than militant. Meanwhile, in both the Delhi Sultanate and the southern states, many Indians crossed traditional religious and cultural boundaries by converting to Islam, making it the second-largest religion in India. Among those attracted to this migrant faith were, again, those of lower castes and the untouchables, and those who sought commercial privileges with Islamic leaders in India or elsewhere in the Indian Ocean region.

After nearly 1,000 years of political fragmentation, India was once again unified under a new wave of Islamic conquerors: the Mughals. The Mughal influence on India was widespread, and they helped to create much of what is today considered Indian culture: the "Mughlai" cuisine of many Indian restaurants, some forms of Indian classical music, distinctive miniature paintings, and such architectural achievements as the Taj Mahal, one of the great symbols of India. Traditionally, these accomplishments were the result of cultural integration. Since Persian was the language of the Mughal court, the culture of Mughal India is described as the product of a Persian-Muslim-Hindu synthesis.

The first Mughal conqueror was Babur who, like many of his predecessors, entered India through the Khyber Pass after establishing a base of power in Afghanistan. Babur was of Central Asian descent, and he claimed both Genghis Khan and Tamerlane, previous conquerors of major empires, as ancestors. His armies entered northern India in 1523, and by 1526, they had conquered Delhi. Babur, himself a devout Muslim, disapproved of the opulence of Indian life but saw that Delhi was an effective base for an empire. In time, his control stretched across the northern part of the subcontinent, from Kabul in Afghanistan to the eastern province of Bengal.

The true architect of the Mughal Empire was Babur's grandson Akbar, who reigned from 1556 to 1605. Unlike Babur, his eyes were set firmly on India rather than on Central Asia or Afghanistan, and he extended the empire by conquering and

Akbar the Great, depicted here with his son Jehangir (left), ruled the Mughal Empire from 1556 to 1605. Akbar increased the size of the empire and created a regime under which all Indians, regardless of religion, were equal.

absorbing Vijayanagar, as well as the province of Gujarat, north of modern Bombay, which gave the Mughals an outlet to the Arabian Sea and a clear route to Mecca in Arabia for Muslim pilgrims. He also solidified Mughal control of Bengal, the rich trade of which offered many benefits and where he placed loyal Muslims as subordinate rulers.

Akbar wanted to create a regime under which all Indians

could live peacefully, regardless of their faith. In so doing, he minimized the significance of the subcontinent's longstanding cultural, religious, and geographical boundaries. Setting the example of religious toleration himself, Akbar married Hindu and Christian wives, in addition to his Muslim ones (under Koranic teaching, Muslim men can take four wives). He also sought out Muslim, Hindu, and Christian cultural advisers, even expressing interest in other Indian faiths such as Parsi (the Indian version of Iranian Zoroastrianism), Jainism (an ascetic faith that was as old as Buddhism), and Sikhism, the new

SIKHISM

The Sikhs are India's third-largest religious group, after Hindus and Muslims. Their religion emerged as an attempt to transcend long-standing borders of religion and caste. During the partition of India, however, the Sikhs found that they, as much as Hindus and Muslims, would suffer from the new arbitrary boundaries.

Guru Nanak founded Sikhism in the early sixteenth century, an era of much creative religious thought in India. His teachings preached equality among all men under a single god, and were especially appealing to peasants, both Hindu and Muslim. This sense of equality was brought into practice in such ways as communal eating, rare in Hinduism, and the release of women from forced seclusion or *purdah*, a Middle Eastern custom brought to India by Muslims, then adopted by Hindus, as well.

Sikhs continue to revere their original ten gurus, the first of whom was Nanak. Amar Das and Ram Das, the third and fourth gurus, enjoyed the patronage of the liberal-minded Akbar, the third Mughal emperor; Ram Das was given a plot of land in the Punjab on which was eventually built Amritsar (the Sikhs' holiest city), to house the Golden Temple. Ram Das's son Arjun, the fifth guru, found himself in trouble during Jehangir's reign; he had supported a rival to the Mughal throne. Jehangir imprisoned him, where he died while being tortured. At this point, the Sikhs turned from being a people who preached peace, as Guru Nanak had taught them, to a militant people, who were ready to defend themselves against any threat.

religion that sought to emphasize what some saw as the best in Hindu and Muslim teachings.

Understanding that the majority of India's people were Hindu, Akbar took special pains to respect their traditions. He worked closely with Hindu nobles and other elites, both to ensure their loyalty and to maintain social order. Many Hindu leaders achieved positions of high responsibility within his administration. Unlike other Muslim leaders, he did not try to convert Hindus to Islam, nor did he charge them the special tax, the *jizya*, permitted under Islamic law. According to historian

Arjun's son Hargobind, whom the Sikhs had pledged to protect, died a peaceful death, although Jehangir's armies forced the Sikhs to retreat to the Himalayan foothills. The seventh and eighth gurus found themselves forced to come to terms with Aurangzeb after the emperor took the throne in 1658, although both died before they faced too much pressure from the new emperor. This was not true for the ninth guru, Tegh Bahadur, who was beheaded by Aurangzeb's men for refusing to give up his faith and was therefore another martyr to the Sikhs' cause.

The tenth and last guru, Gobind Rai, guided the final transformation of the Sikhs into a militant people. He adopted the last name Singh, or "lion," as have all Sikh men in the years since, and described his people as the Khalsa, or "army of the pure." To foster courage, Sikh men developed a distinctive look, so that they could always be identified as Sikhs, and thus prepared to defend themselves in public. Traditional Sikh men never cut their hair, winding it instead in turbans, nor did they cut their beards. They also wore special clothing, carried a small dagger, and sported a silver bracelet around their right wrist. In Gobind Rai's time (1666 to 1708), Sikhs enjoyed little military success against the Mughal armies, but they developed a profound sense of grievance against the Muslim leaders who, since Jehangir's reign in the 1630s, hounded and harassed them.

Stanley Wolpert, "with that single stroke of royal generosity [Akbar] won more support from the majority of India's population than all other Mughal emperors combined managed to muster by their conquests."[5] Akbar could be brutal when necessary; he had secured his authority by throwing a rival out of an upper floor window, then dragging him upstairs and throwing him out again to ensure he was dead.[6] His religious tolerance, administrative reforms, and support for both internal economic development and external trade, though, helped make Mughal India one of the richest, most stable kingdoms on Earth.

The next two Mughal emperors, Jehangir (ruled 1605 to 1627) and Shah Jahan (ruled 1627 to 1657), more or less maintained Akbar's policies of religious tolerance, and they lived lives of opulence along the lines of India's earlier Hindu maharajas, because the momentum of Akbar's administrative reforms continued to keep India stable and prosperous. It was Shah Jahan who built the Taj Mahal as a commemoration to his wife, Mumtaz Mahal. Begun at her death in 1639, the Taj, located in the city of Agra, took 18 years and the efforts of 20,000 artisans and workers to construct. Shah Jahan hoped to build a matching black monument across the Jamuna River from the white Taj as his own tomb, but the last years of his reign were spent dealing with rebellions and wars among his four sons rather than with architectural plans. The Mughals never established firm rules for royal succession, and there were conflicts each time one emperor grew old and his son, or sons, grew impatient to seize power.

Shah Jahan's third son, Aurangzeb, who took the Persian title of Alamgir (World Conqueror), eventually defeated and killed his three brothers and imprisoned his father in Agra's vast Red Fort. Aurangzeb's reign, which lasted until 1707, marked the end of religious toleration in Mughal India. A devout Muslim, Aurangzeb ended the court celebrations—replete with wine, ceremonial elephants, and dancing girls—that had characterized the reigns of his father and grandfather, and he reinstated the jizya, the head tax on "nonbelievers." He also destroyed numerous Hindu temples, banned Hindu festivals, harassed Hindu pilgrims making journeys to sacred sites, and aggressively encouraged conversion to Islam. These steps greatly alienated India's Hindus.

Aurangzeb also spent much of his reign at war, in marked contrast to the reigns of Jehangir and Shah Jahan, which had been mostly peaceful. He briefly extended the empire to its largest size by conquering all of India but its southern tip. The ultimate price, however, was disunity, in effect a return to the subcontinent's age-old pattern. Religious intolerance and the heavy cost of war, which Aurangzeb expected his underlings to squeeze out of their peasants, inspired the emergence of numerous rival kingdoms as new arbitrary borders were drawn. Among these were the Rajputs of India's western regions, a people proud of their prowess in war, whom Akbar had taken special pains to appease, and the Marathas, a new and aggressive military power from the regions along the central west coast. Both the Rajputs and the Marathas were Hindus and found the preservation of Hindu traditions a powerful rallying cry against Aurangzeb's armies.

Another rebel army emerged under the Sikhs in the Punjab. The Sikhs, followers of a faith that drew from both Hinduism and Islam, were originally a people who disdained violence. After suffering oppression under Mughal rulers beginning with Jehangir, the Sikhs were drawn increasingly to warfare to defend themselves and, along with the Rajputs and others, became what the British were later to call one of India's "martial" peoples. Sikh memory, also, is long, and the Sikhs never forgot their sufferings under Islamic rulers.

The Mughal Empire collapsed during the first half of the eighteenth century. Aurangzeb's successors fought among themselves, and some of them, such as the Nizam of Hyderabad, decided to retreat to smaller, more manageable kingdoms. The imperial treasury, also, was depleted, and it was hard to refill when subordinate nobles refused or were unable to pay the necessary revenue. Military challenges, especially from the Marathas, carved away large chunks of territory, and meanwhile, as Mughal authority in the Punjab weakened, the Sikhs established themselves there as a powerful force. By 1757, when British interlopers were about to begin a new stage of history with their own form of Indian imperial unification, the Mughal emperors controlled little except for the city of Delhi itself.

3

Imperial Borders: The British Raj

India was the centerpiece of the British Empire, and in building British India, these foreigners from Europe continued the process of national unification that the previous group of foreign invaders, the Mughals, had begun. From the mid-1700s, when they controlled only a few coastal trading posts, to the mid-1800s, the British cobbled together an Indian empire that consisted, directly, of three-fifths of the subcontinent. Indirect control accounted for the remainder in the form of agreements with India's hundreds of independent princes, who surrendered control of external defense in exchange for economic and other privileges.

The British Empire itself was an entity that by the end of the 1800s encompassed almost a quarter of the world's land mass and included, in addition to India, many and varied territories, ranging from the vast, such as Australia and Canada, to the small but strategically important islands of Hong Kong, Singapore, and St. Helena. Control of the empire had made Britain the wealthiest and most powerful nation on the globe at the turn of the twentieth century, and India was the greatest colonial prize. Lord George Curzon, who as viceroy was the top British official in India from 1898 to 1905, proclaimed, "As long as we rule India we are the greatest power in the world."[7]

For the British, India's importance was strategic, symbolic, and economic. British India prevented other European colonial powers, the Russians or the French, namely, from dominating Asia or the Indian Ocean, and Britain's control over India's vast and diverse population brought great national prestige. India also provided the British with large armies and inexpensive labor, which they exported around the world. Finally, Indian resources such as tea, cotton, and jute helped feed the British industrial machine, whereas the subcontinent provided a huge field for British investors seeking large returns in agricultural or industrial enterprises or markets for their finished goods.

British traders, employees of the English East India Company, first arrived in Mughal India in the early 1600s. Strangely, these traders considered India to be a sort of consolation prize; they had hoped to establish a foothold in the spice trade of the islands of what is now Indonesia, but because of Dutch opposition, they were unable to do so. The Mughal emperor Jehangir granted the British the right to build a trading post in Surat, north of modern-day Bombay, in 1612, and the British impressed the emperor further by pledging to defend the ships of Muslim pilgrims on their way to Mecca in Arabia. Surat was followed by other trading posts, notably Madras (now Chennai), in southern India, in 1640 and Bombay (now Mumbai) in 1674. In 1690, an East India Company employee named Job Charnock established a British station in the province of Bengal, which had large supplies of silk and saltpeter, a mineral used in making gunpowder. This new station, Calcutta (now Kolkata), the site of a deepwater port, was to become the most important British city in India.

By the time Charnock had established Calcutta, the Mughal Empire was collapsing. The emperor Aurangzeb had ended the habit of peaceful coexistence between Muslims and Hindus established by his predecessors, which inspired resistance from a new Hindu force, the Marathas, as well as older ones, such as the Rajputs. He had also embarked on a series of costly wars designed to subdue South India and faced revolts from the Sikhs in the northwest. What resulted was a sort of splintering; although Mughal rule held together in much of India until the 1750s, actual leadership devolved to local kings. As India grew more dangerous and insecure, East India Company officials increasingly found it in their interests to be ready to defend their trade with force. They formed armies officered by British men but made up mostly of Indian troops, and they built fortifications at their trading posts, most notably Fort William in Calcutta.

Administratively, the Company organized itself into three "presidencies"—Bombay, Madras, and Calcutta—each of which enjoyed a high degree of independence from the others. The presidencies were indeed administrative constructs that, on the ground, provided the basis for the Company to establish its geographical foothold in India. The Bombay presidency was the center of trade on the west coast, offering up cotton, indigo (a cloth dye), and spices brought up from the southwest or other places in Asia; at Madras, traders dealt mainly in cotton and sugar, whereas Bengal remained the source of silk cloth and saltpeter.

The three separate Company armies proved useful in the 1740s and 1750s, when the challenge to the Company was not only the continuing decline of Mughal authority but also the presence of the French. France wanted not only to trade in India but also to establish colonies, a move that, at that time, Company officials were consciously trying to avoid, although the expanding cities of Calcutta, Bombay, and Madras made such claims appear to be false. In any case, the Company was afraid of losing its foothold to these aggressive newcomers from France. Since Britain and France were already enemies in a series of European and North American wars, it was no surprise that these conflicts spread to India, with each side using the support or recognition of local Indian leaders in Indian battles. The turning point came in 1757 with a battle at Plassey, west of Calcutta. There, a combined British and Indian force under Robert Clive, who began his career as a clerk in the Madras presidency, defeated a French-led coalition. The Company's reward for this victory, which was accompanied by much meddling with the internal politics of Bengal, was the right to collect revenue throughout the province, which generally took the form of land rents or tariffs on agricultural products. In effect, the Company's armies had become the military of Bengal, one of India's richest provinces, and the Company's representatives now controlled Bengal's internal economy in addition to its external trade.

Many Company employees took advantage of this opportunity, and "the sponsored state became a plundered state," as they sought to enrich themselves as much as possible in hopes of returning to Britain wealthy.[8] In trying to reduce these excesses, the Company found itself forced to put in place a competent civil administration, thereby transforming them even further into the government of Bengal. With no army, and with the Company paying the proper portion of their revenue as tribute

In 1757, General Robert Clive (pictured here) led a combined force of British and Indian troops against the French-supported ruler of Bengal, Siraj Ud Daulah, in the Battle of Plassey. Clive's victory led to his appointment as governor of Bengal, and more importantly signaled the beginning of the English East India Company's control over trade in India.

to the Mughal emperor in Delhi, the local leaders, or *nawabs*, could do nothing in response.

Britain's London-based government, as well as the East India Company's London directors, found themselves forced to adjust to the new circumstances by trying to stabilize the government of the Company's possessions, as well as reduce the worst of the commercial excesses of Company employees. The Regulating Act (1773) named Company official Warren Hastings governor-general and gave him (and his successors) control over Madras and Bombay, as well as Bengal. The 1784 India Act, meanwhile, provided for a Board of Control based in London to oversee the affairs of the British in India. These efforts were not only intended to bring order to the Company's activities in India but also to ensure the continued flow of revenue to the British crown. The London government relied increasingly on tariffs from goods imported by the East India Company, whose trade included not only India but China, as well. The British Empire got its start in this haphazard way, as it came to increasingly depend on the natural resources of areas outside its own borders.

Until 1858, the East India Company acted as the agent of the British government in India, and it steadily gave up its commercial functions to independent *boxwallahs*, or merchants, as it was transformed into a colonial government. Conflicts with Indian leaders, who were often unhappy with the British presence or were seeking to protect or enlarge kingdoms of their own, resulted in wars in the first half of the 1800s. British victories in these wars led to new territorial acquisitions, and these territories were often governed with an orderliness that inspired confidence among Indians. The British indeed redrew the political boundaries of India, but they did little to interfere with most of its cultural and religious ones. As long as order was maintained, and as long as the British did not interfere too much with local or religious customs or the traditional social order, many Indians had little trouble accepting Company rule. They were simply a new set of Mughals. The Company's armies, made up mostly of Indian troops, fought their last series of major conflicts, the Sikh Wars, in the 1840s. Their victories added the Punjab to the Company's possessions and greatly reduced the likelihood of a Russian invasion via Afghanistan. British control of India seemed secure.

By that same period, however, the social contract between British rulers and their Indian subjects had begun to break down; the British broke the agreement through aggressive cultural imperialism by transgressing India's religious and cultural boundaries in ways offensive or intolerable to many Indians. Prior to 1830, the British had taken pains to respect Hindu or Muslim customs, to learn Indian languages, and to try to understand the subcontinent's history on its own terms. It was also common for the British to have Indian wives or mistresses, and a few even took up Hindu or Muslim customs themselves. Officials, together with some Indian reformers, tried to end certain practices they found repugnant, such as *suttee,* the ceremony in which a Hindu wife chooses to join her dead husband on his funeral pyre, but these examples were rare.

After 1830, British reformers were far more aggressive, and so were evangelical Protestant Christian missionaries. They represented the growing sense in Britain that their civilization was not only different from that of India, it was superior. Such reformers rationalized the British presence in India not by citing its strategic importance or economic value, but by explaining that the British were in India to try to raise the level of Indian civilization through their own influence; that part of their duty to India was to impose foreign ideas and institutions. Writer Thomas Macaulay, who served for a time as an East India Company civil servant, asked, "Who could deny that a single shelf of a good European library was worth the whole native literature of India?"[9] As he put in motion plans for educational reform, Macauley ironically suspected that a British-style education, conducted in English, would one day produce a class of Indian leaders ready to govern the country on their own.

Evangelical missionaries found few interested in their doctrines; those who were interested included the untouchable castes or the community of Eurasians, the products of decades of liaisons between Europeans and Indians, who fitted in with neither their British overlords nor with India's many religious or caste groups. Instead, the effect of the missionaries was to alienate many of those with whom they came into contact. The problem was at its worst in the Company's armies. The Bengal Army, attached to the Bengal presidency, which by now stretched all the way across northern India, was in particular made up of Indians for whom warfare was an honorable profession, practiced by their ancestors for centuries. Many of these soldiers, who were broadly known as *sepoys*—although the word technically refers only to infantrymen—were high-caste Hindus, whereas others were devout Muslims. Many suspected that British missionaries, often aided by overzealous British officers, were trying to destroy their ancient traditions. These fears were compounded by many other developments. In an example of the arbitrary destruction of cultural boundaries to which many Indians were subjected to, British land-reform tactics often destroyed traditional relationships between landlords and the peasants who held long-term leases on their lands. Sepoys often found that their families were thrown off the land because of these British reforms and that they themselves were no longer welcomed or respected in their communities. The new attitude of cultural superiority, meanwhile, led the British to treat many Indian kings and nobles with disdain or indifference, and these grievances led to even further disquiet among the sepoys of the Bengal army.

The tension finally erupted in 1857, the year of the Sepoy Rebellion. The event changed the history of British India, and even its name is a source of controversy. For many British people, it was a simple mutiny, centered around rebellious elements of the Bengal Army. For many Indians, the events constituted the First Indian War of Independence, the first concerted attempt to oust European colonialism.

The rebellion was sparked by the introduction into the Bengal Army of a new rifle, the Enfield, which was loaded most efficiently by biting the cap off of a cartridge before putting the cartridge into the weapon. The rumor spread among the sepoys that the cartridges were greased with a combination of pig fat and cow fat. The first is anathema to Muslims, whereas Hindus consider the second a source of pollution. Many units refused to accept the new cartridges, and when one, in Meerut, north of Delhi, was punished harshly for not following orders to use the rifle, many Sepoys decided they had had enough. They rose in rebellion against not only their officers but against all Europeans, and the rebellion spread throughout much of northern India. It began in May 1857 and was not fully subdued until more than a year later.

Both sides committed atrocities. Sepoy murders of British women and children were followed by British calls for bloody revenge, and in the process of reestablishing control, the British sometimes killed entire villages or executed "mutinous" Indians without investigation, much less due process of law. The rebellion did not touch most of India; the Bombay and Madras presidencies were mostly calm. In addition, many sepoys, notably Sikhs, remained loyal to the British. Nevertheless, the atrocities, together with the British arrogance and carelessness that had inspired it, increased the gap between British and Indians, and misunderstanding, distance, and mistrust became the norm.

In 1858, the British government took direct control of India and, soon after, dissolved the East India Company. Britain's Queen Victoria was proclaimed Empress of India in 1877, and the period known as the British Raj, after an Indian term for rule, began. The Raj was governed from London by a cabinet-level secretary of state for India. The chief British official in India itself was the viceroy, the local representative of royal authority. Under him were the various levels of the Indian Civil Service (ICS). At first, the ICS was staffed almost entirely by British officials, with a few Indians serving in low-level positions. Over time, Indians who passed the rigorous civil service examinations were able to reach positions of greater responsibility. The British also maintained an elaborate military structure in India. Despite the 1857 rebellion, most troops continued to be Indians, but they were kept loyal by various organizational means, and the ratio of Indian to British troops was reduced to three to one.

The period of the British Raj, which lasted until India gained independence in 1947, was also the heyday of global imperialism. During the late 1800s, especially, the European powers, together with Japan and the United States, divided much of the world up into far-reaching global empires. Given the competition for colonies that took place, and the imperial expansion of such rivals as France, Germany, and Russia, British leaders considered India, which was the greatest colonial prize of all, more important than ever, and they were determined both to hold it and make use of it.

India remained essential to Britain's economic well-being. It was a major market for exports of both goods and liquid capital, which kept British factories humming and British bank accounts expanding: "By 1913 60 percent of all Indian imports came from Britain and it had absorbed 380 million pounds in British capital, one-tenth of all the country's overseas investments."[10]

Britain's dependence on India as an export market did not benefit the inhabitants of India; local textile weavers and manufacturers, for instance, lost their livelihoods because of cheap cloth imported from Britain. It was a striking transformation, since cloth-making had been one of India's major industries for centuries and Indian cottons had been one of the East India Company's greatest moneymakers in earlier decades. Much cotton cloth was still produced in western India, but the bulk of it was intended for export, usually to other British colonies, and it was produced using British-style plantations and factories. Elsewhere in India, Britain sponsored large-scale agriculture, such as the growing of tea and jute, as well as the construction of factories to process these products. They also crisscrossed India with railroads and telegraph lines, useful for both commerce and administration. Unlike most other colonies during the age of imperialism, British India was designed to pay for itself (without direct assistance from the home government or British taxpayers), and it was largely able to do so.

To assure continued economic benefits, and to discourage further rebellions, the British practiced a version of divide and rule during the era of the Raj, demonstrating that they were will-ing to take advantage of some of the arbitrary boundaries that characterized the subcontinent. India, British administrators understood, featured innumerable divisions of religion, caste, language, and custom, and a gentle exploitation of these differ-ences would help them maintain their authority. One group they favored in particular was the princes, who still controlled some two-fifths of the subcontinent. The greatest princes were showered with British-style honors, such as military appoint-ments, and, in exchange for pledges of loyalty, the British promised the princes that they would not threaten the inde-pendence of their states. Most states simply had to accept the presence of a British "resident," usually a ranking member of the ICS, to provide a means of communication. As British India proper was transformed by industry, and as a very vocal class of independence leaders arose there, the princely states remained relatively backward, but reliably loyal, backwaters. Similarly, the British protected traditional noble landlords, some of whom became vocal supporters of British rule, who ensured that their peasants were both largely docile and consistent in their pay-ments of land revenue.

Other groups the British favored were those who had remained loyal during the rebellion. Here the distinction was clearest in the reorganized British Indian Army. Sikhs, who made up only 2 percent of India's population, made up 25 percent of the army by the 1920s. Other groups that achieved prominence were Pathans, who were Muslims from the Northwest Frontier Province, Gurkhas from Nepal, and the reliable Hindu Rajputs from the regions southwest of Delhi. The troops whose forebears had taken part in the rebellion, namely Bengalis, Biharis, and Marathas, were rarely allowed into the military.[11]

Some anecdotal evidence suggests also that the British favored Muslims over Hindus in general, mostly as a result of closer cultural identification. One British historian wrote of the army that "there was . . . an age-old feeling among some British officers that the Muslim races, with their simplicity of character and directness of speech, were preferable to the Hindus. Tall, upright, uncomplicated, and conservative in outlook, they appeared to mirror British ideals of service and loyalty."[12] This sympathy was not always shared by Muslims, especially Muslim elites, many of whose forebears had been part of India's ruling classes for centuries and who believed, especially in the years immediately following the 1857 rebellion, that the British favored Hindus with university appointments, government jobs, and other privileges.[13]

Britain relied heavily on India during World War I (1914–1918). Hundreds of thousands of Indian troops fought for the British on battlefields stretching from France to Iraq, and India's industrial production helped to feed the home country's war machine. Indeed, the war provided an opportunity for great industrial expansion in products such as iron and steel. Nevertheless, the war proved to be a turning point for British rule in India. Not only did Indian troops expect some sort of recognition for their willingness to sacrifice, but they came home, especially from a Europe full of impoverished peasants and laborers, with strong doubts whether the European way of life was in any way superior to their own. The experience of the war also inspired misgivings about the true nature of British global strength; at one point German ships entered the Bay of Bengal and threatened India itself by shelling Madras.[14] These returning troops, and the people they spoke with at home, began to form a wide audience for an Indian independence movement that was still small in scale.

After World War I, British rule over India began to fray. The British had always recognized that they would not control India forever, but most saw their departure as something possible only in the distant future. After a devastating conflict fought, in the words of U.S. President Woodrow Wilson, to "make the world safe for democracy," though, the existence of autocratic global empires no longer seemed quite as legitimate as before, except to the most devout imperialists.

This new British insecurity was reflected in two sets of laws introduced in 1919. One was the Government of India Act sponsored by the secretary of state for India, Edwin Montagu, and the viceroy, Lord Chelmsford. It provided for greater autonomy for India's provinces, as well as means to elect local Indian leaders for some purposes. The goal was apparently to train both Indian and British officials in the habit of working together, as a prelude to even greater Indian administrative responsibility.

The importance of this promising step was nullified, however, by two Rowlatt Acts, or black acts, named after the judge Sir Henry Rowlatt. These acts extended wartime controls by allowing judges to arrest, detain, and even imprison suspected political troublemakers without jury trials or other regular legal procedures. Judges were not even required to state a cause for arrest. The acts were a major contrast to British legal traditions of openness and due process as understood by many of the nation's independence leaders, who had themselves been trained as lawyers in Britain. The Rowlatt Acts, the source of much fevered discussion and speculation among Indian leaders, were passed into law, but they were never put into effect. One reason was widespread nationalist agitation, which resulted in the most tragic event in the history of the British Raj: the Amritsar Massacre of Sunday, April 13, 1919.

Amritsar, a major city in the Punjab and the Sikhs' holiest city, often had been a center of unrest and communal violence between its majority populations of Sikhs and Muslims. The two communities were united in their postwar nationalist agitation, however, and there were large-scale riots, as well as a couple of assaults on British citizens that April. In response, the British governor-general of the Punjab, Sir Michael O'Dwyer, called upon General Reginald Dyer, an imperialist officer of the old, racist school, to bring troops into the city to enforce martial law and keep the peace. One of Dyer's orders was to forbid large public demonstrations or meetings.

Local Indian leaders ignored the warning and planned a meeting for a large open space known as the Jallianwallah Bagh. The space was traditionally a center for gatherings of various

On April 13, 1919, thousands of Indians gathered during the Sikh religious day of Baisakhi for a peaceful demonstration in the Jallianwala Bagh section of Amritsar in the state of Punjab. Fearing unrest, the local British government sent in troops led by General Reginald Dyer (pictured here) to keep the peace. Dyer, however, ordered the troops to fire on the defenseless civilians and at least 379 people were killed in what became known as the Amritsar Massacre.

kinds in Amritsar, most of them quite peaceful, and hundreds of people went there, many with family members and refreshments, to make a day of it. It was one of the few open areas in the city, and it was surrounded by buildings, with only one major entrance.

Dyer was furious at this flouting of his authority. He surrounded the Jallianwallah Bagh with troops, mostly Gurkhas in origin, and at one point ordered them to open fire. Later investigations indicated that the troops had fired some 1,650 rounds. The official death toll was 379, with 1,500 injured, shocking in and of itself. Most Indian estimates are higher, and they cite not only the large number of rounds fired but the casualties from crowding and trampling, as the panicked crowd tried to escape through the narrow entrance.

The lessons of this tragedy were many, for both British and Indian people. The more perceptive of the British saw this show of force as a sign of failure and came increasingly to conclude that, if India had to be held by force, it could not truly be held at all. Conservative politician and imperialist Winston Churchill, who had no great love of India, called the massacre a "monstrous event" and repudiated the need to resort to force on this scale to maintain order.[15] Alternatively, there were many who supported Dyer's decision and praised him for being willing to take drastic steps to maintain order. After the investigations of the incident, British officials retired Dyer, only to find that his pension was much enlarged by voluntary donations from those who believed he had done the right thing in Amritsar and had been a scapegoat for the British government.

Many Indian leaders saw the Amritsar Massacre as a sign that the British had now lost their moral authority over the Raj. They sensed that the incident had "destroyed the trust in British justice and fair play that had been built up over one and a half centuries."[16] The great Bengali writer Rabindranath Tagore, who had been awarded the Nobel Prize for Literature in 1913 and was subsequently knighted by the British government, returned his knighthood as a sign of his dismay. In his letter to the viceroy, he wrote that

> the universal agony of indignation roused in the hearts of the people had been ignored by our rulers—possibly congratulating themselves for imparting what they imagine as salutary

lessons. . . . The time has come when badges of honour make our shame glaring in the incongruous context of humiliation.[17]

More and more Indians rejected any further British "badges of honour," and the British departure from India was quicker than even most leaders thought it would be in 1919. As India's independence leaders—Mahatma Gandhi, Jawaharlal Nehru, and Muhammad Ali Jinnah—stepped to the forefront, they not only pressed for a British departure but found in the end they had to accept arbitrary borders imposed across India's historic diversity of customs, languages, and religions. Historical circumstances, as well as the desires and actions of individual independence leaders, would determine that, of all of India's diversity, it was to be the differences between Hindu and Muslim that were to be most troubling.

4

The Indian Independence Movement

India gained its independence from Great Britain largely because of a broad-based independence movement. Independence leaders such as Mahatma Gandhi, Jawaharlal Nehru, and Muhammad Ali Jinnah came from a wide variety of backgrounds and represented numerous viewpoints and constituencies. Until the late 1930s and into the first years of World War II (1939–1945), when independence was imminent, these leaders worked side by side, if not always in complete agreement, toward the larger goal of freedom from colonial rule. Only when independence was in sight did some of these leaders envision partitioning India.

The organization that directed the Indian independence movement was the Indian National Congress, or Congress Party. It was formed in 1885 by Allan Octavian Hume, a retired English official dedicated to promoting Indian national self-respect. A total of 72 men attended the congress's first meeting in Bombay in December 1885, and, over the subsequent years, branches of the Congress Party emerged in major cities throughout the country. Its leaders tended to be young Indian men from wealthy backgrounds and many had been educated in Britain. They included high-caste Hindus, as well as Parsis, descendants of Persian Zoroastrian immigrants who had prospered under British rule. In time, Muslim leaders also cast their lot with Congress.[18]

Congress's initial goal was to provide a forum by which Indian leaders could communicate their concerns and grievances to the colonial government, and it maintained that role until independence came in 1947. By the turn of the century, however, congressional leaders openly advocated self-rule. Some, such as Gopal Krishna Gokhale, preached patience, but others, notably Bal Gangadhar Tilak, were more inflammatory in their criticism and threats. Tilak cited evidence of British misrule, such as poor handling of a famine that killed millions in the 1890s, and asked, "what people on earth, however docile, will continue to submit to this sort of mad terror?"[19]

A misstep by the viceroy, Lord Curzon, in 1903 gave the Congress Party much fuel for their fire. A hint of things to come,

Lord George Curzon, who served as viceroy of India from 1898 to 1905, presided over the partition of the province of Bengal in 1905. However, due to mass dissent, especially by the Hindus of eastern Bengal, the partition was rescinded in 1912.

Curzon made a decision to partition the province of Bengal, a vast territory which at the time included not only Bengal itself but also Bihar to the west and Orissa to the south, as well as other territories. Curzon's concerns were administrative; he simply believed the province was too large and populous to run effectively, and he thought it might make sense to partition the province along some, though not all, of its standing linguistic and cultural lines. In doing so, though, he wildly underestimated the dissent that the move would inspire from various groups, such as the Hindus of Muslim-majority eastern Bengal, who might suffer from it. Congress was able to use the nationwide protests that followed the announcement of partition, in December 1903, to invigorate their movement, citing British arrogance and misunderstanding of Indian problems and concerns. Although congressional speechmakers called for a national *swadeshi* ("of our own country") movement, others prepared for more direct action, in the form of a nationwide boycott of imported goods.[20]

The boycott was a major success, at least among Hindus. Muslim leaders chose not to support it, as the swadeshi movement took on an increasingly Hindu tone, with demonstrations often overlapping with Hindu festivals. One Muslim response was the formation of the All-India Muslim League, in December 1906. The League's purpose was to protect the political rights of Indian Muslims, but always with an eye toward working with the British government, as well as with groups representing other communities.[21] Both the swadeshi movement and the rise of the Muslim League had some effect; in government reforms passed in 1909, Indian councils were established that gave various constituencies representative voices in both the provincial and national governments. In a manifestation of Britain's divide-and-rule tactics, Muslims gained disproportionate representation in these councils and had fewer restrictions on their right to vote.[22] Meanwhile, the partition of Bengal was rescinded, although Bihar and Orissa were combined to create a new province. King George V made this announcement during a 1911 visit to India. He followed it up with the proclamation that the British national government would be moved from Calcutta, the commercial capital and center of Hindu nationalism, to the traditional capital of Delhi.

Soon afterward, the independence movement was transformed by the return to India of Mohandas Gandhi, who is far better known as the Mahatma, or "great soul," a title given him

by the Nobel Prize-winning Bengali writer Rabindranath
Tagore. Born in 1869, Gandhi had trained as a lawyer in
London. Unable to find sufficient employment after his return
to Bombay as a young man, he moved to South Africa, a British
colony which contained a large community of Indian migrant
laborers. There Gandhi found his calling, defending local
Indians against the "color bar" that stood between both Indians
and native Africans and the European community; it was a key
example of the British employing their standard divide-and-
rule tactics in another of their diverse territorial possessions.
On the intellectual level he believed profoundly in nonviolence
and religious toleration. But he was also a clever political tacti-
cian who recognized the importance of such abstractions as
moral authority. To establish the latter, he devised a set of techniques under the name *satyagraha*, a word translated variously
as "love force" or "truth force." These techniques required passive resistance and the readiness to accept punishment in the
attempt to turn your opponents' mind and heart toward truth
and away from injustice.

Ordinary Indians were drawn to Gandhi in ways unavailable
to the rich, anglicized lawyers who dominated the Congress
Party, and it was he who turned Indian independence into a
mass movement. In writings and speeches, Gandhi emphasized
the subcontinent's common heritage rather than its divisions,
and millions of Indians responded enthusiastically to his efforts
to downplay traditional cultural boundaries. He also advocated
simple living and the craft-based village economy, often visiting
villages to stay with ordinary peasants and learn of their problems and concerns. He wore only a spare white loincloth made
from cloth he had woven himself, and ate a meager diet. He also
focused his energies on India's downtrodden groups, notably the
untouchables, whom he dubbed *harijans*, or "children of God."

Gandhi returned to India in 1915, and quickly became active
in congressional politics, as well as efforts to uplift the lives of
the poor through such actions as strikes. In the turmoil of India
following World War I and the 1919 Amritsar Massacre, in

which overeager British officials killed hundreds of Indians attending a peaceful meeting, Gandhi made his first important national moves. The 1920 Non-Cooperation Movement, approved by Congress, was a nationwide set of demonstrations and boycotts that, Gandhi believed, would lead to independence in 1921. To the Mahatma's despair, however, the demonstrations deteriorated into violence and political disagreements and he himself was thrown into prison by British authorities, a common experience for him.[23] Nevertheless, the movement had turned him into a national hero and, as congressional leaders soon after rejected their suits and ties for simple white clothes made of khadi, or homespun cotton, he invented the symbolism of the independence movement as well.

Ready to make another attempt at a national satyagraha effort after the failures of the Non-Cooperation Movement, Gandhi called in 1930 for a nonviolent attack on one of the symbols of British colonialism: salt. The British had maintained for decades a monopoly, on salt, a commodity everybody needs, and they charged heavy taxes on its sale and use. In defiance of this monopoly, Gandhi staged his famous salt march, an event which gave him true international fame. Beginning at his ashram, or spiritual center, in Ahmedabad on March 12, 1930, Gandhi and his followers walked 250 miles to Dandi, on the west coast, north of Bombay. There, he stepped into the coastal marshes and picked up a piece of sea salt, demonstrating that, in effect, salt simply lay there for the taking, that it was absurd for a foreign government to control its use. At Dandi, and indeed, all along the route, news cameras and reporters accompanied the marchers, who in time numbered in the thousands, and they sent their reports back to a fascinated world. Hoping to avoid publicity, British officials did not interfere with the march itself but in the days afterward, and at night, they arrested Gandhi and he was led to prison once again.[24]

By this time, a new generation of practical politicians had arisen to guide the Congress Party. Prominent among them was Jawaharlal Nehru. Nehru, who was to later serve for 17 years as

India's first prime minister, was the son of Motilal Nehru, an Allahabad lawyer also prominent in the Congress Party. Descended from Kashmiri Brahmins of Hinduism's highest caste, Jawaharlal was not religious and was in fact more comfortable speaking English than any Indian language. In the years following World War I, he fell under Gandhi's influence and supported the independence movement's new emphasis on ordinary Indians rather than anglicized elites. Charismatic and humanistic, Nehru also had the gift of agreeableness; he was able to get along on a personal level with congressional officials who differed widely on tactics and goals, and ordinary people respected him as well. Nehru was elected president of Congress in 1929, and at that year's congressional meeting, the assembled representatives declared that their only goal was to gain complete independence, or *swaraj*, for India, not a half-measure such as self-rule within the British Empire. Gandhi wrote the declaration: "We believe that it is the inalienable right of the Indian people, as of any other people, to have freedom and to enjoy the fruits of their toil and have the necessities of life, so that they may have full opportunities of growth."[25] Leaders also unveiled the congressional flag, a tricolor of three stripes: orange for Hindus, Green for Muslims, and white to represent peace and unity. At this stage it had the Gandhian symbol of a spinning wheel at its center.

Other congressional leaders who rose to importance during the 1920s included Vallabhbhai Patel, Muhammad Ali Jinnah, and Subhas Chandra Bose. Patel was a Gujarati lawyer skilled in hard-nosed, grassroots politics, and in organization building and fund-raising. Muhammad Ali Jinnah was the most prominent Muslim in the Congress Party. Uneasy about the prospect of continued Hindu-Muslim unity, Jinnah was also prominent in the Muslim League, an organization that for most of the 1920s and 1930s was moribund. Bose, who came from an important Bengali family, was ready to reject Gandhi's calls for nonviolence in search of more militant tactics.

The tide was turning, and Indian leaders increasingly set the agenda. In the words of one historian, post–World War I British officials had "lost the touch of Empire, and far from commanding events, bemusedly responded to them."[26] The 1927–28 Simon Commission, which tried to explore constitutional reforms, included no Indian leaders and was soundly rejected by Congress. In 1931 Gandhi, released from prison, traveled to London to take part in discussions designed to give further freedoms to Indians. No agreements were reached, and any that were could not have been binding, since Gandhi did not represent Congress's Central Working Committee. The main effect of his visit was to further burnish his international reputation. Gandhi stayed in the poor quarters of London's East End and, even in the cold of September, wore only his loincloth, even to visits with British leaders. Conservatives, who then controlled Britain's government, were not impressed. One of them, empire advocate Winston Churchill, was dismayed that "this one time Inner Temple lawyer, now turned seditious fakir, [was] striding half-naked up the steps of the Viceroy's palace . . . to negotiate and parley on equal terms with the representative of the King-Emperor" on his return to India.[27]

Back in India, the apparently inexorable movement toward independence continued, and various groups began jockeying for representation and power in negotiations over a possible constitution that would subsume India's traditional divisions within the framework of a modern nation-state. Now that independence had become a foreseeable reality, Indian leaders found it necessary to consider these practical questions. Muslim leaders such as Jinnah had already proposed forms of proportional voting for their community. Now, in the early 1930s, other groups stepped forward. These included the Sikhs, Eurasians, Indian Christians, and Untouchables, whose leader, Dr. B. R. Ambedkar, was both clever and formidable. These negotiations, and continued British stonewalling, resulted in further demonstrations and other forms of political action, and Gandhi as well as Nehru and other leaders were in and out of prison with some regularity. A few members of a reinvigorated Muslim League, meanwhile, had proposed that, once independence came, India be partitioned into two states: one for Hindus and a second, to be named Pakistan, for Muslims. Jinnah, at first, did not take the proposal seriously, nor did Nehru. As for Gandhi, he was horrified at any consideration that India be partitioned.

As the momentum toward independence continued—for example, Indian membership in the Indian Civil Service reached 50 percent by the early 1930s—the British government produced two Government of India Acts. The first, in 1935, satisfied few Indian leaders, since it "loosened British authority in India, but did not altogether remove it."[28] The proposal would have created an awkward Indian Federation consisting of eleven "Indian" provinces, the princely states, and a number of other provinces managed by the Indian Civil Service. At the very least, this Act was a hint that India's best hope for unity was through a federal system in which states and provinces enjoyed a measure of freedom from any central government.

A turning point arrived in 1937 with a second Government of India Act. A complicated arrangement of provincial governments was retained from the 1935 Act, as well as a system of proportional electorates representing the various communities. The key to the 1937 Act, however, was elections. The electorate was "expanded to include some thirty-five million propertied Indians, six million of whom were women, and 10 percent untouchables."[29] As a result of the elections, the Congress Party took over the governments of seven of eleven Indian provinces, with an eighth added in 1938. It also cemented its status as India's great majority party, winning 70 percent of the popular vote.

The Muslim League, now the second most powerful party but still garnering less support than Congress, found itself sidelined. The new Congress Party's provincial governments openly favored Hindu officials and took advantage of such trappings as Hindu festivals, songs, and processions. Many Muslims feared that the British Raj was now likely to be replaced by a Hindu Raj, which would dominate all minority groups, and that their concerns would be ignored and their people oppressed. Muhammad

Ali Jinnah, seeing his opportunity, broke from the Congress Party and pledged to turn the Muslim League into a mass movement. If an independent India was going to be governed by a Hindu Raj, then the only true alternative for him was to support a separate nation—the Pakistan that he had rejected earlier. Nehru and Muslim leaders in Congress, such as Maulana Azad and Abdul Ghaffar Khan, top official in the Northwest Frontier Province and a close associate of Gandhi, scorned Jinnah's fears. Congress, they claimed, contained tens of thousands of Muslim members and represented all of India, not only its Hindus.[30]

In any case, Congress did not accept its new responsibilities with complete grace. Governing responsibilities opened up tempting avenues for corruption, and many top officials lacked experience in practical governance. Another problem was Subhas Chandra Bose, the president of Congress. Bose was popular with younger and more radical congressional members, but the old guard, notably Gandhi, was unhappy with him. In the 1938 presidential election among the All-India Congress Committee, neither Nehru nor Patel were ready to stand, leaving the door open for a less experienced candidate. Bose went on to win the election but, due to Gandhi's objections as well as the resignations of important members, resigned his office in February 1939. Bose broke from Congress to form the Forward Bloc, a party ready to use radical techniques, even revolutionary violence, to gain freedom. Bose himself took the title Netaji or, simply, "leader."

World War II in Europe began on September 1, 1939, when Adolf Hitler's German armies marched into Poland. Great Britain followed with a declaration of war on Germany and, on September 3, the viceroy of India, Lord Linlithgow, informed India that it, too, was now at war with Germany. Congressional leaders were outraged at not having been consulted. At the very least, they wanted the opportunity to bargain for complete independence as a condition for India's involvement, but that opportunity was denied them. In protest, congressional officials resigned from their posts in provincial governments, a step

Jawaharlal Nehru (left) and Mohandas Gandhi enjoy time together during an All-India Congress Committee meeting. Neither Nehru, who was elected India's first prime minister at this meeting in 1946, nor Gandhi supported the partition of India.

which angered British officials who thought they had already made major concessions to Congress and who now had a major war to fight. Jinnah took advantage of this discord by making stronger calls for Pakistan and, in March 1940, at the annual meeting of the Muslim League in Lahore, the League pledged that a Muslim nation was indeed their main goal.[31] Over the successive years, and by largely staying out of the conflicts that enveloped Congress and the British, Jinnah achieved the tacit support of the British for the partition of India, generally in the form of an expressed need to strongly consider Muslim interests in any independence negotiations.

Congressional leaders still rejected the notion of partition, and elected the Muslim Maulana Azad as party president to reflect their belief that Congress represented India's Muslims, as well as its other groups. Meanwhile, the vicissitudes of war further lengthened the gap between congressional leaders and the British, whose main priority was victory over the Germans and their Japanese allies, not intransigent, squabbling Indian politicians. The British did not appreciate Gandhi's new efforts at passive resistance in 1941 and threw many resistors into prison. They were released, however, when Japanese advances in China and Southeast Asia put India itself at risk for invasion. Netaji Subhas Chandra Bose, for his part, escaped first to Germany, then to Japan, where he started the buildup of an Indian National Army (INA) made up of captured Indian soldiers from Britain's colonies of Malaya, Burma, Hong Kong, and Singapore, all now under Japanese control.

Hoping to secure India's support for the war, the British wartime government, under Winston Churchill, sent Labour leader Sir Richard Stafford Cripps to offer an independence deal in March 1942. Because it would have allowed provinces and princely states to opt out of any independent India, and since it put off full independence, Congress leaders rejected it outright. Gandhi sent Scripps home with the phrase that his offer was simply "a post-dated check on a bank that is obviously failing" ringing in his ear.[32]

Congress soon after adopted the Quit India campaign, which began formally in May 1942. Under Gandhi's guidance, officials asserted that Britain and India no longer had any common interests, and that it was time for Britain to leave. Unable to tolerate this during a dangerous war, the British reacted strongly. Gandhi, Nehru, and other leaders were once again imprisoned, along with tens of thousands of other Congress activists, and demonstrations and riots followed in many cities. As he had discovered earlier, Jinnah figured his best course was to stand aside, condemning Congress for troubling Britain in its hour of danger and refining his calls for an independent Pakistan.[33]

At the end of World War II in 1945, India was much transformed. War needs had expanded India's industrial base until it rivaled that of any nation outside of Western Europe, North

America, or Japan. Indeed, the Jamshedpur iron and steel complex under the control of the wealthy Tata family "was the largest single producer of steel in the British Empire."[34] In addition, the wartime need for grain, cotton, and other commodities added wealth to India's agricultural communities and made many people rich, although mismanagement and poor planning had also led to a famine in Bengal in 1943 and 1944. This famine killed millions and gave further credence to the belief that Britain had lost its moral authority to govern. The presence of easygoing Americans, there to help stop the Japanese advance, had also given Indians confidence, because America, now the world's greatest power, was opposed in principle to colonialism, and its people were not afraid to say so. Early in World War II, but before the United States entered the war, Winston Churchill, now Britain's prime minister, met with U.S. president Franklin D. Roosevelt, and the two devised the Atlantic Charter. The Charter called for "the right of all peoples to choose the form of government under which they will live."[35]

Although Churchill later said that the words did not, at that time, apply to India, his prime ministership did not outlast World War II in Asia. His replacement, Clement Attlee, was ready to give India its independence quickly and to work with India's leaders to accomplish it. These leaders, after much negotiation and conflict, and in the midst of a rising tide of communal violence, were to decide to partition India; to create arbitrary borders that would divide its two largest religious groups, Hindus and Muslims. This concern was to outweigh all other considerations of economic ties, security concerns, or the needs of the region's other religious, cultural, or caste minorities.

5

Negotiating
New Boundaries

In June 1945, with the support of millions of soldiers eager to return to civilian life, Clement Attlee, the head of Britain's Labour Party, was elected prime minister, ousting wartime leader Winston Churchill. In principle, labour leaders were committed to Indian independence, in stark contrast to Tories like Churchill, who wanted to preserve India as the centerpiece of the British Empire, not only because of its economic and strategic importance but as a matter of national pride. Labour also understood that Great Britain, exhausted and financially drained from years of war and depression, and with a population clamoring for its troops to be brought home, could no longer afford to maintain arbitrary borders worldwide.

The form that an independent India was to take, however, was a troublesome and complicated question, one about which British and Indian leaders held different and often contradictory views. The issues were many. One was whether India would become a truly independent, sovereign nation or remain a dominion, a new member of the British commonwealth of nations that included such "white" dominions as Australia, New Zealand, and South Africa. Another was the issue of federalism, or the relationship between national and regional governments; by 1945, India's provinces, such as Bengal and the Punjab, already enjoyed a great deal of autonomy and were governed by local councils made up of Indian politicians.

Still another concern was the status of the princely states, relics of earlier epochs of Indian history that remained in place into the twentieth century, nominally free from British control. In 1945 India, there were 562 princely states, governed by absolute monarchs who bore such titles as maharaja, raja, or nizam. Some were no larger than a few square miles. Others, such as Hyderabad, were nearly as large as Britain itself. Altogether the princes ruled two-fifths of India's territory and held sway over a quarter of its people. Still another important question was the status of minority groups such as Sikhs, Indian Christians, or the much larger groups of low-caste or untouchable people as defined by Hindu tradition.

As it happened, it was the question of India's largest minority group, the Muslims, that was to prove decisive. There were some 92 million Muslims out of a total Indian population of about 400 million. Their leaders had long served in the Congress Party, the organization that guided the independence movement, and many individuals, such as Maulana Azad, president of Congress from 1940 to 1946, were more than willing to work closely with Hindu leaders in the process of ousting British rule and constructing a modern nation. Their standpoint was that, in an independent India, Hindus and Muslims would coexist more or less peacefully, as they had for centuries, provided Muslims had proper representation in national and local governments and their rights were protected under law. This seemed the most reasonable possibility, in large part because Muslims were scattered throughout India rather than concentrated in certain regions. Indeed, only in Bengal, in the northeast, and the Punjab and other provinces in the northwest, did Muslims make up around half or more of the population. Muslim leaders could also point to a long tradition of importance in the country; Muslim emperors were the dominant rulers of most of India from 1106 to 1757.

Notwithstanding their demographic dispersal, and the accommodative opinions of leaders like Azad, some Muslims thought that their interests and traditions might best be protected if they had a nation of their own rather than a kind of "protected minority" status in a nation dominated by Hindus. The idea of an independent Indian Muslim state was first spoken aloud, in a meaningful context, in 1931 at the annual meeting of the Muslim League, the organization that had emerged to protect Muslim interests in the independence struggle in 1906 and whose power and influence waxed and waned in the years since. Indeed, in 1931, the role of the Muslim League was at a low ebb. Nonetheless, at that meeting, the League's acting president, poet Muhammad Iqbal, announced that "the formation of a consolidated North-West Indian Muslim State appears to me to be the destiny of the Muslims, at least of North-West India."[36]

Two years later, in 1933, a group of Muslims living near

Britain's Cambridge University took Iqbal's suggestion further. They published a pamphlet entitled *Now or Never,* in which they not only proposed the boundaries of an Indian Muslim state, they also gave it a name: Pakistan. Claiming that he was inspired by God, or Allah, the group's guiding light, Choudhary Rahmat Ali, asserted that the new state should consist of the areas of the Punjab; "Afghania," or the Northwest Frontier Province; Kashmir; Sind; and Baluchistan; all in India's northwest. From these names, Ali derived the name "Pakistan." This word also connoted "the land of the pure," because *pak* is a word signifying ritual purity in Urdu, the language of India's Muslims. Ali also proposed that Pakistan have close relations with two other possible independent Indian Muslim states: Hyderabad, which might be renamed Usmanistan in honor of its ruling dynasty the Usmans, and Bang-i-Islam, carved from the northeastern provinces of Bengal and Assam. Rahmat Ali's viewpoint was an extreme notion shared by some mainstream Muslim leaders in India; that the independence movement's leaders in the Congress Party, mostly Hindus themselves, were seeking to replace the British Raj with a Hindu one. Wrote Rahmat Ali, "we will not crucify ourselves on a cross of Hindu nationalism."[37]

In the 1931 meeting, Muhammad Iqbal had been standing in at the request of the Muslim League's president, Bombay lawyer Muhammad Ali Jinnah. Jinnah was born in Karachi, Pakistan's first capital, in 1876, although his family had originally come from the princely state of Kathiawar in the western region of Gujarat, which was incidentally also the ancestral home of Mahatma Ghandi. Educated in law in London, Jinnah joined the Congress Party in 1906, while working in that city. After relocating to Bombay, and showing great promise as both an attorney and politician, Jinnah rose to become a member of Congress's Supreme Legislative Council. He joined the Muslim League in 1913. At this early stage, Jinnah numbered among the moderates of the Indian independence movement and certainly evinced no interest in a separate Indian Muslim state. For more than two decades, in fact, Jinnah was at the forefront of the effort to

Muhammad Ali Jinnah, pictured here in 1947, was elected president of the Muslim League in 1916. Although he originally supported independence for a unified India, Jinnah gradually came to realize that British oppression would be replaced by Hindu oppression of the Muslim minority, and thus he supported an independent Pakistani nation.

ensure that Muslims and Hindus remained united in their effort to oust British rule. He went so far as to announce in 1933 that Pakistan was an "impossible dream."[38]

The pressure of events was to change Jinnah's mind. He resented the power of Mahatma Ghandi, considering him an overly clever, attention-seeking rabble-rouser, and he was particularly concerned that Ghandi seemed to want an independent

India dominated by Hindus. Despite the Mahatma's statements of religious and cultural toleration, Jinnah thought that Ghandi's lifestyle, his panoply of resistance activities, and his appeal to millions of ordinary Hindus had the effect of relegating Muslims to India's margins, and by the mid-1930s, Jinnah had the growing concern that Ghandi's Hinduizing was carrying congressional leaders like Jawaharlal Nehru, Subhas Chandra Bose, and Vallabhbhai Patel with him. Although it had always been dominated by Hindus numerically, Jinnah slowly became convinced that Congress was truly only acting in the interests of Hindus.

The major turning point for Jinnah came in 1937. On April 1, nationwide elections for local governing councils took place. Although these elections confirmed that India's provinces would have a large degree of autonomy, the elections also demonstrated the electoral power of Congress; the party won 70 percent of the vote and established governments in seven provinces. The victory was so sweeping that Nehru, in one of his numerous instances of rhetorical excess, announced that "there were only two parties in India—the [British colonial] government and the Congress."[39]

Jinnah refused to accept the implied argument that the Muslim League was now irrelevant or that he, as its leader, had no more than a marginal role to play in Indian politics. Consequently, he set about turning the League into a well-supported mass movement. In this, he was apparently helped by the actions of Hindu politicians after they took office in their provincial councils. According to India historian Stanley Wolpert, Hindu leaders had sought power for so long that, now that they had it, they behaved with an understandably high level of eagerness. They placed cronies and family members in important positions, listened more to the grievances of Hindus than others, and in some of the trappings of office—flags, anthems, public celebrations—they seemed to emphasize Hindu traditions and desires. All of this allowed Jinnah and other Muslim leaders to charge Congress with bias against Muslims and to use that charge to attract widespread public support.[40]

Jinnah had great success. By the end of 1938, he had managed to unite all important Muslim parties under the League's umbrella, building a political force big enough to potentially challenge Congress. Nehru and the others refused, however, to accept Jinnah's claim that it was now the League that spoke for India's Muslims, citing the fact that there were tens of thousands of Muslim members of Congress. Congress leaders were also hesitant to accept either a political challenger or a divided Indian voice in negotiations with the British.

The political borders were now drawn, but it was the events of World War II that solidified the split between Congress and the Muslim League, and it was the stubbornness of Muhammad Ali Jinnah that ensured the League was committed to partition. Both Congress and the League used their support for the British war effort as a bargaining chip; many congressional leaders insisted that the price of their support would be an independent India. By contrast, Jinnah, as always, played his cards close to the vest and, in negotiations, always held out for more. He set a drastic line from the beginning, although he was careful to avoid any serious suggestion that Indian Muslims did not support Britain in the war. At a meeting of the Muslim League held in Lahore in March 1940, Jinnah convinced the league to agree on a so-called "Pakistan Resolution," arguing in support of the notion that "if the British government is really in earnest and sincere to secure peace and happiness of the people of the subcontinent, the only course open to us all is to allow the major nations separate homelands by dividing India into autonomous national states."[41]

Jinnah's appeal was based on the common world-wide conception of the late 1800s and the first half of the 1900s, that "nations" were not simply political entities but groupings of people united by language, religion, custom, ethnic background, and other factors. Therefore, India's Muslims constituted a "nation" that was identifiably separate from the Hindu "nation," and Indian Muslims could not hope to have their interests truly protected by Hindu leaders. Gandhi disagreed with this conception, claiming that Indian Muslims were descended from Hindu converts to Islam or were converts themselves, and they therefore remained fundamentally Indian. Jinnah considered Gandhi's argument ridiculous and overly sentimental, given the Mahatma's desire for a united India, and rejected it.

Jinnah had now set the terms, and as Indian Muslims came increasingly to agree with them, Congress and the British had to adjust. In fact, in the days after the Lahore conference, outgoing British Secretary of State for India Lord Zetland told the House of Lords that "a united India could only be achieved through agreement between the Indian communities, and that Britain could not force a constitution on the Muslims."[42] Meanwhile, Zetland's replacement, Leo Amery, was of the opinion that, given the urgency of the war, Indian independence should be achieved as quickly as possible. Britain's role was to act as an agent in this process, and increasingly, as a mediator between Congress and the Muslim League, between Nehru and Gandhi on the one hand and Jinnah on the other.

Congressional leaders further turned the negotiating tide in Jinnah's favor with certain developments during World War II. Congress rashly supported the Quit India movement of 1942, a nationwide series of strikes and demonstrations that followed the failure of a British mission, led by Sir Stafford Cripps, to open independence negotiations. British leaders, who refused to consider granting full independence while fighting a war, responded by imprisoning most congressional leaders as well as tens of thousands of their supporters. Meanwhile, former Congress president Subhas Chandra Bose left India and formed an Indian National Army from captured prisoners of war. He hoped to use it, with Japanese sponsorship, in a war of independence against Britain and its allies. Although Congress leaders largely repudiated Bose, the renegade enjoyed a great deal of support among the rank and file of the party.

Jinnah, for his part, stood aloof from these goings-on and remained free to play his hand carefully and skillfully. He demonstrated that the idea of Pakistan had the sort of mass support that neither Congress nor the British could ignore, for instance, by staging mass meetings on "Pakistan Day," 1942, the second anniversary of the Lahore meeting. He also avoided any activity that might suggest the League sought to hinder the British war effort; indeed, Indian Muslims (as well as Hindus and Sikhs) served by the tens of thousands both in India itself, which was under threat of a Japanese invasion, and in Europe and Southeast Asia. Further, he was so effective at negotiating that he was able to convince Amery and two British viceroys, Lord Linlithgow (who ruled from 1936 to 1943) and Lord Wavell (who ruled from 1943 to 1947), that Congress was, in fact, incapable of

THE INDIAN NATIONAL ARMY

During World War II, the Bengali politician Subhas Chandra Bose, who had served a term as the president of the Congress Party, actively sought the support of the Japanese in trying to forcefully end British rule in India. Already in voluntary exile, he formed the Indian National Army (INA), made up of Indian troops whom the Japanese captured during their conquests of British colonies in Hong Kong, Malaysia, Singapore, and Burma. Ultimately containing more than 25,000 Indian troops, many of whom were uncertain about its purpose, the INA was armed and trained by the Japanese army, and Bose's hope was that it would fight alongside the Japanese in an invasion of India. During the INA's only major military operation, when Japanese and INA forces mounted an attempted invasion of northeastern India in March 1944, thousands of troops deserted to the British side of the lines. Other congressional leaders, such as Jawaharlal Nehru, openly repudiated the INA.

At war's end, the British took about 23,000 members of the INA prisoner but could not hope to try them all. In fact, as the Indian independence movement accelerated, many Indians, including Nehru, were sympathetic to the former INA troops, criticizing their judgment but praising their nationalism. The British settled for trials of three of the top INA officers, one each from the Hindu, Muslim, and Sikh communities. The officers were defended at their trials (held in late 1945), however, by a group of prominent Indian lawyers, representing the interests of all Indians despite its stubborn assertions, and that the Muslim League was the true bargaining agent representing the quarter of India's people who professed Islam. In time, congresionals leaders, seeking independence above all and unable any longer to resist either Jinnah or the British willingness to listen to him, were forced to accept the notion that the Muslim League had to be a factor in any independence negotiations. This meant in practice that they had to deal with Jinnah, and that they had to accept at least the possibility of partition and the creation of Pakistan.

Negotiations proceeded haltingly, with decisive moves often being made through less than formal means, because many

including Nehru himself. The three officers became national heroes, and demonstrations filled the streets in their support. "Netaji" Bose, or the "leader," saw none of this, having died in an airplane crash in Taiwan while on his way to Tokyo on August 17, 1945.

Discontent also filled the standing British Indian armed forces, which had been greatly enlarged during World War II with soldiers who now demanded to be demobilized and allowed to go home. There were brief incidents of unrest at several Royal Indian Air Force bases in early February 1946 and a large-scale mutiny in the Royal Indian Navy (RIN) that began on February 18. The mutiny spread to 78 ships and a number of shore installations, and those involved demanded that the British go home and other grievances be addressed. In Bombay, the RIN's major western port, the mutiny inspired massive demonstrations of support in the streets. It only ended after congressional leaders, who condemned the event, promised that the mutineers would not be punished and after loyal troops, as well as ships of the British Navy itself, appeared in Bombay. After the mutiny, the British sent out a Cabinet Mission of top officials to draft a plan for India's independence, now fairly certain that India could not be held much longer. The actions of the INA as well as regular armed forces units showed that the most important border in India now separated the Indians from the British.

congressional leaders remained in prison. In April 1944, Chakravarty Rajagopalachari, a close associate of Mahatma Gandhi and a lower-ranking Congress Party member, proposed to Jinnah that, if the League supported Congress in its demands for independence, his reward would be the acceptance of the principle of Pakistan; the actual issue to be decided in postindependence votes in Muslim majority areas in northeastern and northwestern India. It was a major victory for Jinnah, the first open acknowledgement by a prominent congressman that Pakistan might now be acceptable.

As World War II came to an end a year later, the viceroy, Lord Wavell, freed congressional leaders from prison and brought them, along with Muslim League officials, to a conference at Simla, the hot-season retreat of the British government. The meeting took place in June 1945, just prior to the British election that sent Clement Attlee to the prime minister's office. Wavell's brief was to discuss the formation of an interim government that would in time accede to Indian independence. The attempt failed largely because Jinnah refused to accept the political status of Maulana Azad, the Muslim president of the Congress Party, and argued further that no Muslim leader could have any standing unless he was a member of the League. The British government refused to hold Jinnah responsible for his intransigence, strengthening his hand even further by demonstrating that they did not really expect him to offer concessions to Congress, and in so doing, "made Pakistan virtually inevitable."[43]

The Muslim League strengthened its electoral position, as well, with a successful showing in the first postwar elections. In late 1945, League candidates won all of the Muslim seats in the national Central Assembly. In provincial elections held in February 1946, League members took almost all the available Muslim seats and were able to lead coalition governments in two provinces. His power confirmed by these successes, Jinnah maintained a strong hand in the tortuous negotiations of the successive months, his stubbornness sometimes tempered by his close associate and chief lieutenant, Liaquat Ali Khan.

On March 24, 1946, a British cabinet mission, sent out to help Indian leaders devise an independence plan, arrived in Delhi, India's capital. The mission was partly an acknowledgment that the Indian question had to be settled quickly, because authority seemed to be fraying and the country seemed destined for unrest. One clear sign of this situation was a mutiny in the Royal Indian Navy in February 1946, which involved one quarter of the total number of Indian sailors. Although the mutiny itself ultimately fell apart, "both the [British] government in Delhi and Congress were stunned by the mutiny which seemed to suggest that the authority of both might be on the verge of disintegration."[44]

By early April, the cabinet mission's leader, Sir Stafford Cripps, concluded that only two solutions might be accepted by both the Muslim League and Congress. Both were implicit acknowledgments of Pakistan. Cripps's Plan A called for a small centralized government coordinating an "All-India Union" divided into Hindu majority areas, Muslim majority areas, and the princely states. Plan B partitioned India into Hindustan and Pakistan, leaving the princely states free to choose whether to join either or remain independent. The British government agreed with Cripps's proposals, which nevertheless left one of the pressing questions of any partition plan unresolved: Would the mostly Muslim provinces of Punjab in the west and Bengal in the east be given to Pakistan, or would these two areas, rich in agricultural land and home to the important cities of Lahore and Calcutta, be divided? Jinnah's negotiating position for years had been that he would not accept divisions of the Punjab and Bengal; such a concession would amount to a "moth-eaten Pakistan," unable to support itself economically and therefore not viable as a sovereign state.[45] However, when Cripps and Wavell met him to discuss Plans A and B on April 16, Jinnah was noncommittal, refusing to state his opinion until he heard that of Congress. Jinnah likely realized that he was not going to get

Prior to partition, British Labour politician Sir Stafford Cripps (pictured here) developed two plans for an independent Pakistan. Cripps's Plan A called for a small centralized government divided into Hindu majority areas, Muslim majority areas, and the princely states; while his Plan B called for the partitioned area to be divided into Hindustan and Pakistan, leaving the princely states free to choose whether to join either or remain independent.

everything he asked for but that Pakistan, his overall goal, was now quite possible. Partition of Bengal and the Punjab might be the necessary price.

After another meeting with Wavell and Indian leaders at

Ambala in May 1946 failed to result in a satisfactory compromise, the Cripps cabinet mission published a recommendation based on the earlier Plan A and the ideas of Maulana Azad. The result came to be known as the Cabinet Mission Plan, and it provided both partition and foundation of an agreement that was to lead to India's independence. The plan proposed an Indian Union with a limited central government and two groups of provinces in which mostly Muslim regions would enjoy self-governing status. The princely states would be forced to cede elements of their authority to the central government. The plan rejected the notion of a completely independent Pakistan, arguing that a nation made up of two pieces separated by 700 miles was an unrealistic possibility, although the plan left open the possibility of provinces opting out of the Indian Union in years to come. Given this provision, Congress labeled the deal "the plan to get Pakistan by the back door."[46] Prior to the implementation of the plan, an interim government would take office and begin to write a new constitution for this All-India Union.

Jinnah signaled his acceptance of the plan, since its details ensured that Muslim regions would enjoy a great deal of autonomy; indeed it seemed the next best thing to actual independence, which might itself become possible after some years had passed. He was also sure that he and the League would enjoy great influence in the interim government. In fact, he reached a side agreement with Wavell that would have permitted the League itself to form an interim government in the event that Congress rejected the plan. Gandhi, seemingly never satisfied, nearly scuttled the plan, insisting against reasonable wisdom that Indian independence be declared prior to the writing of a constitution or the meeting of an interim government and that British troops leave the country. Still, on June 25, Nehru, Patel, and Azad sent word that, "with serious reservations about the limitation of the central Authority," they nonetheless accepted the plan.[47] The Scripps mission returned to London, hopeful that they had finally carved out an arrangement acceptable to both Congress and the League.

This moment of hope was dashed when, at the All-India Congress Committee meeting held in early July to provide for the replacement of Azad by Nehru as president, Nehru announced that Congress was "not bound by a single thing" in the plan.[48] In fact, and despite its prior statements, congressional leadership feared that the plan ceded too much power to the Muslim League and a weak central government was too risky. Jinnah, in response, pulled back. He saw Nehru's statement as a humiliating and an unacceptable response to the Muslim League's gains, and when British officials, seeking to defend Nehru and Gandhi, watered down the League's power even further in the proposed interim government, the Muslim leader reacted strongly, calling for direct action on the part of India's Muslims. The long months of communal violence, in which hundreds of thousands of ordinary Indians were killed, were set to begin.

Following a fiery Bombay meeting in which he addressed some 450 League members, Jinnah reasserted that he was now no longer willing to accept anything less than a fully sovereign Pakistan, a measure that was supported unanimously by the assembled members. Arguing that he and other League members had done everything in the power to negotiate in good faith, only to be betrayed by a hair-splitting, inconsistent Congress, Jinnah declared that it was time to place negotiations on the back burner. He announced that August 16 would be "Direct Action Day" across India. Muslims would use Ghandi's old techniques of civil disobedience, notably the *hartal*, or complete stoppage of work and other activity, to shut down the country and make their grievances known. Proclaiming, "We now bid goodbye to constitutional methods. . . . There is no tribunal to which we can go. The only tribunal is the Muslim nation," Jinnah took the Pakistan movement to the streets.[49] In Calcutta, demonstrations disintegrated into riots and, over several days, 5,000 people were killed and tens of thousands more injured, while perhaps 200,000 refugees either fled the city or sought safe quarters within its limits, their shops and homes destroyed or no longer secure. The violence threatened to spread to other cities, and public rhetoric grew increasingly heated: "from Dacca [in the east] to Peshawar [in the west] people prepared to kill or be killed, in the cause of Kali or at the bidding of Allah. 'We shall have India divided,' wrote Jinnah, 'or we shall have India destroyed!' 'I tell the British, cried Ghandi, 'give us chaos!'"[50] Although Calcutta ultimately calmed down, the killings were only a sign of events to come.

On August 27, 1946, after a personal visit to a devastated Calcutta, Wavell met with Nehru and Ghandi. The viceroy was convinced that only a solid constitutional agreement between Congress and the Muslim League could save India from disaster, and he reiterated British support for the Cabinet Mission Plan. Nehru and Ghandi continued their prevaricating, however, and when Wavell grew angry, the Mahatma, the renowned advocate of nonviolence, declared that "If India wants her blood-bath, she shall have it."[51] Wavell, an old soldier rather than a politician or lawyer, set about preparing to remove British citizens from India in the event of a civil war or a complete breakdown of civil order.

An interim government was duly formed on September 2, 1946, as Prime Minister Attlee and his advisers in London insisted the Cabinet Mission Plan go forward despite Jinnah's rejection of it and the continued threat of communal violence. Nehru took office as vice president of the government's executive council; in effect he was India's prime minister, subordinate only to the viceroy. Vallabhbhai Patel, a hardliner with regard to the Muslim League and partition, was named home secretary, responsible for, among other matters, internal security, whereas the top military official was to be the Sikh Baldev Singh. Muslims, meanwhile, saw the occasion as one for mourning. They flew millions of black flags on September 2, setting off another round of communal violence, although a less dramatic one, centered in Bombay.[52]

By mid-October, Wavell finally convinced Jinnah to allow the League to join the interim government now that it was an accomplished fact. The Muslim leader refused, however, to serve in it himself, unwilling to accept a position subordinate to that of Nehru. Instead, the chief League official in the interim government was Liaquat Ali Khan, who held the office of finance minister. Altogether, League members held 5 of the 14 cabinet posts. Still, the interim government never functioned as an effective coalition, and Liaquat Ali's bloc generally met independently of the other ministers. Since he controlled the public purse, it was easy for him to interfere with the government's business. For an old hand like Jinnah, Liaquat's tactics of stonewalling and obstruction simply constituted another form of negotiation.

As 1947 approached, there seemed little hope of a peaceful settlement; communal rioting threatened to break into open civil war in both Bengal and the Punjab. A final meeting of principal leaders in London in December 1946 produced no new compromises, and the Cabinet Mission Plan was finished. Nehru flew home from London to announce that "we have now altogether stopped looking towards London."[53] Attlee, meanwhile, decided to replace Wavell with Lord Louis Mountbatten and to set India on a rapid course to independence despite the lack of a definite plan. Thinking that a clear deadline would force all parties to act with a proper degree of urgency, Attlee announced that Britain would leave India in June 1948.

Mountbatten arrived in India on March 22, 1947, and began to use his considerable charm, which only Jinnah remained immune to, in order to forge a compromise. Talks with all important leaders, as well as the need to solve the problem quickly, convinced him by mid-April that Pakistan was inevitable. Congressional leaders were coming to the same conclusion, wondering whether a united India containing millions of recalcitrant Muslims was worth the trouble. According to historian Percival Spear, "Jinnah's intransigence had won the day. He had already paid a big price and was to pay a bigger. He had succeeded in presenting the Congress with the choice of Pakistan or chaos. Only Gandhi was willing to face chaos."[54]

Jinnah, for his part, realized during his frequent meetings with Mountbatten that he had won what he wanted: an independent

Pakistan within the British Commonwealth, and that since the previous summer "he only had to keep arguing to ensure that Pakistan came into being."[55] Liaquat Ali came to similar conclusions. Although many details remained to be settled, and the partition settlement had only begun to take its toll in bloodshed, the two leaders and their Muslim League colleagues could now prepare to take power in a new nation, to be carved in some form from the Muslim-dominated provinces of northeastern and northwestern India. This impractical, improbable nation, Jinnah's "impossible dream" of 1933, was about to become reality. The modern concept of "nation," which claimed that nations were made up of peoples sharing common cultural, linguistic, religious, and historical ties rather than a common piece of territory, had triumphed. The support for a separate Pakistani "nation" was so strong that it led to the creation of arbitrary geographical boundaries that were made up of two widely separated pieces, or "wings."

6

Drawing
Arbitrary Lines

The last British viceroy of India was Lord Louis Mountbatten, who was known as "Dickie" to his friends. A member of the British royal family, cousin to King George VI, Mountbatten was dynamic and ambitious, and during World War II he had risen to the post of Commander in Chief of Allied Forces, Southeast Asia. A naval man, his chief career goal was to become Lord Admiral of the British Navy, a post that had been denied his father during World War I because of the family's German background. In addition to his other qualities, Mountbatten was charismatic and handsome, and his stock was raised further by his marriage to Edwina, an intelligent and driven woman in her own right. Still in his mid-40s at the end of World War II, Mountbatten was at the leading edge of a rising generation of British officials and politicians, and both he and Edwina developed a close relationship with Jawaharlal Nehru, India's first prime minister.

Mountbatten was hesitant to accept the post of Viceroy of India when it was first offered to him by Prime Minister Clement Attlee in January 1947. He feared that the situation in India, then threatening to descend into widespread rioting if not outright civil war, could only turn out badly, and he did not want to damage his reputation by presiding over a desperate British departure. He was only convinced to take the post after a conversation with his cousin the king and after Attlee agreed to grant him almost unlimited powers to organize the transition to Indian independence. Attlee, for his part, was happy to agree. He wanted someone in India with Mountbatten's drive and stature to replace the well-intended but pessimistic and introverted Lord Wavell.[56]

Mountbatten was sworn in as viceroy on March 24, 1947. He tried to get the situation in hand quickly by arranging face-to-face meetings with top Indian officials, thinking that this personal approach might work better than arranging meetings with all present, which had a history of ending in stalemate. For the rest of March and into the first weeks of April, Mountbatten held a number of meetings with top Congress Party officials

Jawaharlal Nehru and Vallabhbhai Patel, as well as with Muslim League leaders Muhammad Ali Jinnah and Liaquat Ali Khan. He also met with Mahatma Gandhi, the symbolic head of India's independence movement, who at that time was concerned about both the growing violence in India and the apparent likelihood that the country would be divided. These meetings convinced Mountbatten that the partition of India was now the only realistic possibility left if Britain was to achieve its goals; Jinnah was simply too set in his conviction to see Pakistan become a reality, and Nehru and other Indian leaders were unwilling to grant concessions to Jinnah or his Muslim League that might prevent or delay partition. Britain's goals were a peaceful withdrawal and the assurance that India and Pakistan remained tied to their soon-to-be-former colonial overlord by accepting membership in the British Commonwealth of Nations. Mountbatten's charisma was such, and his arguments forceful enough, that even the hesitant Patel agreed to accept the principle of partition. Only Gandhi continued to resist the idea, but he had no official post in the Congress Party or India's interim government, so his objections had no binding force on the decisions of others.

The agreement that Mountbatten hammered out with India's leaders was dubbed "Plan Balkan" by members of the viceroy's staff who likened it to the divisions of southeastern Europe in the years before World War I. During those territorial divisions, the Turkish Ottoman Empire, which had dominated the regions of southeastern Europe known as the Balkans for several centuries, retreated. It left behind a complex patchwork of ethnicities and religious groups that, in that sense, was similar to India. Some of these groups, such as the Serbs, aggressively pursued nationalist interests, whereas others sought simply to preserve a sense of territorial or cultural integrity. The conflicts that arose in the Balkans in the late nineteenth and early twentieth centuries were some of the prime causes of World War I. Mountbatten's staff feared that the "Balkanization" of India would prove violent, as well. One of these administrators, Chief of Staff Lord Ismay, later wrote, "No one in India thought it was perfect. Yet nearly everyone agreed that it was the only solution which had any chance of being accepted by all political parties, and of ensuring a fairly equitable deal for all minorities. It was not a gamble. There was no other way."[57] Plan Balkan went through several drafts before Krishna Menon, a congressional civil servant, devised a solution that satisfied Mountbatten's insistence that India remain within the British Commonwealth. Menon's proposal was that both India and Pakistan become immediate Commonwealth members and that India's many princely states, rather than becoming independent, would join either India or Pakistan. It was, in effect, an acknowledgement that the partition of India was imminent.[58]

Mountbatten approved of the plan and set out to convince Nehru and Patel of its merits. Both had come around to accepting the principle of partition, but, perhaps impatient to actually govern after years of struggling for independence, they hesitated to remain closely tied to Britain. Jinnah had fewer such qualms, as he recognized that Commonwealth status would enable Pakistan to maintain strong military ties to Britain. Once Nehru was reassured that the plan would not permit individual provinces to break away from India beyond Pakistan, he pronounced himself satisfied. Patel, whose political arm-twisting would secure the support of the entire Congress Party, agreed to it on the condition that Britain leave India quickly, well before the June 1948 deadline announced by Attlee.[59] Plan Balkan had now become Plan Partition.

On June 2, the viceroy convened a meeting of important Indian leaders, whose number included the Sikh representative Baldev Singh but not Gandhi, although the Mahatma later turned up on his own. It was the first such gathering of importance since December 1946. There, Mountbatten secured Jinnah's public rejection of the 1946 Cabinet Mission Plan, which would have left India united. After all the principals left to consider the partition plan once again, Mountbatten met with Jinnah, where with some difficulty he got the Muslim League leader to stop his

On June 2, 1947, Louis Mountbatten (center), vice president of India's interim government, met with Jawaharlal Nehru (left) and Muhammad Ali Jinnah (right) to discuss Britain's plan for the partition of India. Shortly after the meeting, Mountbatten secured Jinnah's support and within ten weeks, both nations had achieved independence.

endless negotiating and acquiesce to the partition plan as it then stood. The deed was done. Mountbatten had already secured the agreements of congressional leaders and the Sikhs. His final gesture at the meeting was to present Indian leaders with a prepared document entitled "The Administrative Consequences of Partition." It required them to face the practical consequences of their decision, to "unravel the web left behind by three centuries of common habitation of the subcontinent"[60]—three centuries, that is, of British presence, in which most of the unraveling would be practical and administrative: the divisions of government offices and property, the national debt, and the armed forces. For many Hindus and Muslims, ties dating back ten centuries would have to be sundered, and many of these ties were abstract yet still vital, notably the connection of villagers to their surroundings and to neighbors who practiced a different faith.

The partition plan, meanwhile, became public knowledge on June 3, but it did not specify precisely where the actual borders of India and Pakistan would be.

In a press conference, Mountbatten announced that the date of Britain's departure would not be June 1948, nor sometime near the end of 1947, as he had originally thought. It would be August 15, 1947, two years after Japan's surrender ending World War II. On July 4, the official Indian Independence Bill was presented to the British Parliament; London having had to scramble to make Plan Partition and the August 15 deadline official. The British pronounced themselves quite pleased with events; one, Lord Samuel, said that "it may be said of the British Raj as Shakespeare said of the Thane of Cawdor, 'Nothing in his life became him like the leaving of it.'"[61] Even Conservative leader Winston Churchill, who had announced in 1931 that to leave India would mean the end of the British Empire, gave his assent to the plan, and it passed into law on July 15. London's leaders seemed to have little comprehension of the chaos their quick departure would cause. Meanwhile, in Delhi, Mountbatten printed up hundreds of large tear-off calendars to be placed in government offices, each new page noting that India was one day closer to independence.

The quickness of Britain's departure left little time to accomplish the practical aspects of partition now that the ideal had been achieved. India's governmental assets had to be separated, its civil service divided, its armed forces split, and, most importantly, borders had to be drawn. None of these tasks were accomplished without conflict or misgivings or, in the case of the borders, great violence. Adding even greater risk to the plan was the fact that India "would simply take over a going concern with everything in place. Pakistan, on the other hand, would be starting from scratch, without an established administration, without armed forces, without records, without equipment or military stores." [62]

Commissions and committees came up with formulas to divide government property, and the concerned officials were so conscientious that they worried about every railroad car, filing cabinet, desk lamp, and even the instruments in police bands. After much discussion, both sides agreed on a 1 to 4 ratio for government property. For cash assets and their counterpart, the national debt, the ratio was 82.5 percent for India and 17.5 percent for Pakistan.[63] Government employees, meanwhile, generally remained in their places across the subcontinent or, if they worked for the central administration, made a choice between India and Pakistan. Establishing these arbitrary boundaries was reasonably straightforward, if not without conflict.

The division of India's armed forces was more troubling for those directly involved and provided a clear example of the arbitrary borders being drawn. Although material assets, such as guns and ships, were divided on the same ratio of other government property, the same could hardly be done with the soldiers. Most troops were reassigned based on religion, a task fraught with difficulty, since, for example, many Muslims did not want to go to Pakistan, and other troops were neither Muslim, Hindu, nor Sikh. Many troops felt that their loyalty to the armed forces and to their comrades was more important than their communal ties, and they did not want India's new borders forced upon them. Meanwhile, officers were given the choice of either the Indian or Pakistani armies; most Hindu and Sikh officers chose India, but for Muslims the choice could be very difficult. Many Muslim officers had families and other ties to India and did not wish to uproot themselves. Others felt loyalty above all to Indian Muslims and the ideal of Pakistan, and they hoped to carry the traditions of the Indian army into the new country. These officers made their choices but, in some cases, brothers found themselves in separate armies, which, within months, were to oppose one another on the battlefield. Their fellow Hindu or Sikh officers, meanwhile, were often just as distressed at the very idea of partitioning a force that had served India and the empire loyally for decades and had managed to remain aloof from politics.

Mountbatten's plan had made no provision for any specific

borders between India and Pakistan. No one had. All anyone knew was that Pakistan would have two "wings," an eastern and western, separated by hundreds of miles of Indian territory. They also knew that, as part of the agreements tentatively reached already, the eastern province of Bengal would be divided, and so also would the western province of Punjab. Jinnah was forced to accept what he had earlier argued would be a "moth-eaten Pakistan," shorn of some of the economic assets of the two provinces: part of the rich agricultural lands of the Punjab, as well as the Bengali city of Calcutta.

The divisions of Bengal and the Punjab were about as arbitrary as they could possibly be, the only guideline being to separate areas of dominant Hindu or Muslim populations. To draw the borders, Mountbatten organized two boundary commissions, one each for Bengal and the Punjab. At their head was a prominent London lawyer named Cyril Radcliffe. He knew almost nothing of India, which was one reason he was chosen for the task and flown to India on July 8. Mountbatten and other officials thought that his ignorance of India would allow him to act without prejudice toward either side.[64]

Radcliffe's commissions met in a heavily guarded bungalow on the grounds of the viceroy's mansion in Delhi. The Englishman worked with eight prominent Indian judges, four each chosen by Congress and the Muslim League. To his despair, Radcliffe quickly found that the principle of drawing borders based on population concentrations could hardly be done clearly or evenly; Hindus, Muslims, and Sikhs (who mostly hoped to live in India) were simply too dispersed. Some areas had a clear majority, but in thousands of villages, especially in the Punjab, Hindus, Muslims, and Sikhs had lived side by side for centuries. Inevitably, large numbers of people were going to find themselves placed in countries where they did not wish to live or where they might not be welcome.

The potential borders might also give rise to devastating economic effects. The Punjab was watered by the Indus River system, which flowed down from the Himalayas in the north.

Complex irrigation networks using these waters had turned the Punjab into the most agriculturally rich part of India. Any new borders would not only cross the rivers, they would also split irrigation networks; a water pump that fed Indian fields, for instance, might be placed in Pakistan, making the entire system virtually useless. The economic vitality of eastern Pakistan was also in danger, although the drawing of the border there was generally more straightforward than in the Punjab. Eastern Bengal's main product was jute, a natural fiber used to make bags and other packaging materials. Most of the jute was processed in factories in Calcutta. If the boundary commissions decided to award Calcutta to India, millions of jute farmers would lose their livelihoods, turning eastern Pakistan into the rural slum that many feared. Meanwhile, pending any new arrangements, thousands of Calcutta factory workers might be made idle and therefore a potential threat to civil order.

The partition of the Punjab presented a particular danger to the Sikhs. They made up only 2 percent of India's population, but the Punjab was their traditional homeland and was where most Sikhs lived. Drawn to the armed services, Sikhs had served in numbers disproportionate to their total population in the armies of British India, and a military leader named Baldev Singh had served as both the representative of the Sikhs and of the military during the independence negotiations of previous years. Their martial tradition derived, in part, from their perceived need to defend themselves from Muslim kings whose habit of oppressing Sikhs dated back to the seventeenth century. The Sikh population, one-sixth of the total, was scattered throughout the Punjab, and the area had been the home of an independent Sikh kingdom during the early 1800s.

Sikh concerns were not at the forefront of Radcliffe's boundary commission, whose borders were mostly based on Hindu or Muslim interests. Sikhs in the western Punjab feared that the new borders would place them in a Muslim state where they would face renewed oppression in a repeat of earlier patterns of Muslim-Sikh hostility. Militant Muslims, meanwhile, had little interest in seeing a large Sikh population maintained in western Pakistan. The situation was ripe for conflict and misunderstanding, especially as both Muslims and Sikhs began to take up arms to defend themselves or to plunder the other. One of Radcliffe's few clear choices was to award the city of Amritsar, the site of the Sikhs' Golden Temple and their holiest spot, to India.

Some Sikhs lived in India's princely states, and the Sikh Maharajah of Patiala was the head of the Council of Princes that had represented the states in India's independence negotiations. The princes were very concerned to preserve at least some of their authority and privileges after independence. Many claimed that, since the British had entered into separate agreements with each of them, their states should return to full independence once the British had left. Neither Nehru or Jinnah had sympathy for these arguments, and Mountbatten was not about to let the question of the princely states slow down the rapid march toward independence. Plan Partition required the princes to choose either India or Pakistan and be forced to sign articles of accession in each case, giving up any claim to political power. In exchange, the princes could keep their titles and a portion of their estates, which were sometimes vast and extremely wealthy. Groups of diplomats traveled to visit each of the princes, and by early August, almost all of them, recognizing the inevitable, had signed the accession documents. Three holdouts remained. One was the Nizam of Hyderabad, reputedly the richest man in the world. He controlled a state that was nearly as large as Britain and theoretically wealthy enough to survive on its own. He was a Muslim prince, however, in a state populated mostly by Hindus and one that would be landlocked, surrounded by India, once independence occurred. Another holdout was the ruler of Junagadh, a small state on the coast, north of Bombay. The third hesitant prince was the ruler of Kashmir, Hari Singh. His indecision, and Kashmir's strategic importance, led to the first armed conflict between India and Pakistan in the fall and winter of 1947.

Meanwhile, Radcliffe's boundary commissions proceeded

throughout July and early August with their unhappy task. They finally presented their boundary awards to Mountbatten on August 13, and Radcliffe, under heavy guard, returned to Britain, where he remained haunted by his decisions until his death. Mountbatten decided to tell nobody of his partition plan, not even Nehru or Jinnah, before independence had been accomplished.[65] He feared not only escalating communal violence, but that news of the specific borders would dampen enthusiasm over the coming independence celebrations, when any troubles would be the responsibility of the Indian and Pakistani governments, not the British one. He kept the newly drawn borders

TERRITORIAL LOOSE ENDS

India still contained territories controlled by others when it became independent in August 1947. Since Jawaharlal Nehru and other Indian leaders wished to consolidate their new nation and prevent any fragmentation, they had to find ways to incorporate these territories and ensure both that India's new territorial boundaries were secure and that further fragmentation would not occur.

Three princely states remained independent that August, their leaders refusing to accede to India, even though most of their counterparts had already done so. One of these was Kashmir, which only acceded to India under the threat of an invasion from Pakistan and whose status is still a source of conflict. The other two required drastic action by India's government. One, Junagadh, was a small state on India's western coast, north of Bombay. Its prince, a Muslim, wanted to cede his state to Pakistan, even though Pakistan lay some 150 miles away and most of Junagadh's population was Hindu. Nehru's government mounted a naval blockade of the coastal kingdom and, in October 1947, sent in an army of 20,000 to take control of the state by force. The prince exiled himself to Pakistan, and Junadagh's accession to India was legitimized by a vote among its people in 1948. It was integrated into the state of Gujarat.

Hyderabad, a large and wealthy kingdom that possessed, among other features, its own currency and its own airline, proved more troublesome. Its locked in a safe in his office and diverted any complaints from Indian or Pakistani officials on the matter.

Radcliffe had been unable to justify awarding Calcutta to East Pakistan, given the importance of the city to recent Indian history. Moreover, it contained large populations of Sikhs, Hindus, and other religious groups. He placed the border of East Pakistan just to the east of the city itself, leaving the region without a major city. Calcutta governor H. S. Suhrawardy and other separatists thought, even in the spring and summer of 1947, that East Pakistan should become an independent country. In a clear example of creating new troubles by determining arbitrary

leader, the Nizam-ul-Mulk, wanted to remain completely independent of both India and Pakistan. When the Nizam refused to give up his independence, Nehru and his deputy prime minister, Vallabhbhai Patel, granted him a period of one year, until August 1948, to change his mind. After the year had passed and the Nizam still had not given in, the government authorized a large-scale invasion that resulted in four days of fighting and a victory for India. Hyderabad and nearby territories became the Indian state of Andhra Pradesh.

Other parts of India still remained under the control of European colonial powers. In the south near Madras was Pondicherry, a possession of France since the seventeenth century. Realizing that there was little point to maintaining such a small outpost against the desires of India, the French relinquished it peacefully in 1954. France had already, in 1951, surrendered its other outpost: the settlement of Chandernagore in the suburbs of Calcutta.

On India's west coast was the large Portuguese enclave of Goa, the oldest European possession in India. Nehru began negotiating with Portugal's military government soon after independence, but the Portuguese did not want to give up an enclave that they had held for more than 450 years and that was once the center of their Asian empire. Fed up, Nehru sent in the army in 1961. The Portuguese were unable to mount any effective resistance over several days of fighting, so Goa became part of India, as did Portugal's other small outposts, Daman and Diu, north of Bombay. Both Goa and Pondicherry were made Indian states and retained a distinctive, part-European character.

boundaries based on stated religious affiliation alone, Bengali Muslims had little in common with Muslims in the Punjab or other western provinces; indeed, aside from their religion, they were little different from Bengali Hindus, with whom they shared the Bengali language and numerous customs. Jinnah himself, meanwhile, had never even visited eastern Bengal, and it remained separated from Pakistan by hundreds of miles. Still, neither Jinnah nor Nehru was willing to accept partition into three rather than into two, and they completely rejected calls for Bengali independence.

The boundary awards in the Punjab gave the city of Lahore, one of India's largest, to Pakistan, whereas Amritsar, only 40 miles away, remained in India. Elsewhere, the line was fairly arbitrary. Radcliffe and his advisers used the only available maps, which were old and outdated, and despite a few visits and flyovers, he gained very little accurate sense of Punjabi topography. Sometimes, not only villages, but farms and even houses were separated by the blunt axe that severed the Punjab. In a last-minute decision that was to have far-reaching consequences, Radcliffe awarded the district of Gurdaspur to India. Gurdaspur provided the only reliable land route connecting India to Kashmir. Had the district instead been awarded to Pakistan, it is likely that Hari Singh, Kashmir's maharajah, would have had no other choice but to cede Kashmir to Pakistan as well.[66]

With the boundary set and the plans protected, Mountbatten prepared for the final withdrawal of Great Britain and the independence celebrations of India and Pakistan. One concession he had had to make on the deadline was to shift it to August 14 rather than August 15. Hindu astrologers had pronounced August 15 to be an extremely inauspicious day and, in a nation where people consulted astrologers for important decisions on matters ranging from marriage to starting businesses to going to war, such opinions mattered. Astrologers determined that the August 14, however, would be auspicious, and independence ceremonies were scheduled for midnight on that day.

On August 13, Mountbatten and his wife traveled to Karachi,

the city proclaimed the capital of Pakistan. They were met there by Jinnah, who had been unanimously elected president, or head of state, by Pakistan's constituent assembly on August 11, and the two traveled by open car to recognize the new nation's independence. Jinnah's lieutenant, Liaquat Ali Khan, was to be the nation's first prime minister and as such, the head of the government. Mountbatten later remembered being rather nervous because of rumored assassination attempts, but Jinnah maintained his customary cool and aloof demeanor. Pakistan's independence celebrations were as elaborate as could be expected, but Karachi had few facilities appropriate for large celebrations, or even for large-scale governmental administration. This left most of the celebrating to cheering crowds in the streets, which the two leaders' car passed through.[67] Karachi, a city of 350,000, was overwhelmed by the 250,000 visitors and migrants who had arrived to witness the independence celebration and to shout again and again, *Pakistan Zindabad!* or "long live Pakistan!" Mountbatten gave Britain's farewells to the assembled representatives of Pakistan's diverse peoples in the crowded—and heavily guarded—assembly hall that had been chosen for the occasion. He was followed by Jinnah, who thanked Mountbatten and the British and expressed his certainty that the two nations would remain on good terms. Jinnah had made a more dramatic speech on August 11, before the constituent assembly. There, he proclaimed that Pakistan would be a nation of complete religious freedom and tolerance, not the Islamic state that many feared. He ensured his people that "my guiding principle will be justice and complete impartiality, and I am sure that with your cooperation, I can look forward to Pakistan becoming one of the greatest nations of the world." [68]

India's formal independence celebrations began at sundown, when a procession of Hindu sannyasin, or holy men, presented a collection of sacred symbols to Jawaharlal Nehru, designated India's first prime minister, at his Delhi home. Also that evening, Great Britain's flag, the Union Jack, was struck from flagstaffs at military and government posts around India for the last time. As in Karachi, hundreds of thousands of celebrants and migrants converged on Delhi to witness the celebrations firsthand, whereas millions of others readied festivities of their own in India's cities and villages.

At midnight, after India's constituent assembly had been sanctified by further Hindu rites and after a choir had sung the Congress anthem "Vande Mataram," ("I Bow to Thee, My Motherland"), a Sanskrit poem whose adoption had angered Muslims earlier, Nehru rose to speak. His speech, delivered extemporaneously and without notes, and delivered across India via the radio, announced: "Long years ago we made a tryst with destiny, and now time comes when we shall redeem our pledge, not wholly or in full measure, but very substantially. At the stroke of the midnight hour, when the world sleeps, India will awake to life and freedom." [69] Soon after, India's new flag, a tri-color of orange, white, and green, was raised at Delhi's red fort, an edifice originally erected by the Mughals. The Gandhian spinning wheel that had graced the banner earlier was now replaced by a sign reflecting a much earlier symbol of India's heritage: the Ashokan Buddhist wheel of life. India had achieved independence. The planned processions of Nehru, Mountbatten, and other leaders through Delhi's streets the next day proved impossible. The crowds were too thick and, to many people's surprise, both exuberantly happy and peaceful.

At 5:00 P.M. on August 16, Mountbatten revealed Radcliffe's boundary awards to India's and Pakistan's leaders—Jinnah and Liaquat Ali Khan had flown into Delhi for the occasion. None were pleased. The placements of Calcutta, Lahore, and Amritsar were no surprise, but other issues inspired ill feeling. Baldev Singh was dismayed that so many Sikh holy places had been awarded to Pakistan. Indian leaders were unhappy that the mostly Buddhist Chittagong hill tracts, in far eastern Bengal, also went to Pakistan.[70] Jinnah, for his part, was disappointed that Gurdaspur District, which again provided India's only road link to Kashmir, went to the Indians, despite an earlier warning to Mountbatten's staff that "this would have a most serious

Residents of Calcutta, India, celebrate their country's independence in mid-August 1947. Within weeks of the announcement, 11.5 million Muslims and Hindus headed toward either Pakistan or India.

impact on the relations between Pakistan and the United Kingdom."[71] Radcliffe had apparently based his Gurdaspur decision on Nehru's desire to leave Kashmir connected to India pending the decision of the hesitant maharajah, Hari Singh, to join one of the two new nations.

The borders were revealed to the public on August 17, and those Punjabi villages whose residents had cautiously flown both Indian and Pakistani flags on August 15 now knew their status. The immediate effect was to vastly increase a torrent of migration toward India or Pakistan that had begun already. Within weeks, 11.5 million people were on the move. Ten million of these were in the Punjab, as 5 million Hindus and Sikhs made their way toward India and a similar number of Muslims headed for Pakistan.[72] These millions were people who had found new arbitrary borders drawn around them, often with little attention paid to tradition or other communal relationships, or to areas that had served the agricultural needs of its inhabitants for generations. The migrations were accompanied by communal violence that left hundreds of thousands dead. V. P. Menon, a member of Congress who had played a large part in refining the partition plan and convincing many of India's princes to accede to it, said simply as India became independent, "now, our nightmares really start." [73] He seemed to understand that the drawing of new national boundaries did not automatically create viable new nation-states, especially in a land as diverse and complex as India, a land where people's loyalties might be attached as much to a religious community, caste, cultural group, or village as they were to a traditionally defined nation-state.

7

Building a Legacy: The Partition Riots

Many Indians and Pakistanis, especially those from the Punjab, associate independence and partition with forced migrations, loss of property, and death. This legacy is one of the reasons why the two nations have maintained a bitter distrust of one another in the years since 1947. Some 11.5 million people migrated between India and the two "wings" of Pakistan in 1946, 1947, and 1948, and of those, 10 million were from the Punjab. The pattern was for Muslims to depart for Pakistan and for Hindus and Sikhs to leave the newly designated territories of Pakistan for India. The process was far from peaceful, and estimates of those killed range from 200,000 to over one million. Sometimes the scenes of killing in these partition riots were so horrific that even hardened military men and war correspondents were stunned. *New York Times* reporter Robert Trumbull wrote: "I have never been as shaken by anything, even by the piled-up bodies on the beachhead at Tarawa [a bloody World War II battle]. In India today blood flows oftener than the rain falls."[74] Women and children were not spared and were sometimes killed by family members wanting to save their loved ones from defilement.

India's religious diversity had periodically inspired violence in the subcontinent's history, although incidents were usually fairly small in scale and localized. Aside from overt periods of oppression, such as the late 1600s, when the Mughal Emperor Aurangzeb, a devout Muslim, directly targeted Hindu and Sikh practices and customs, the general pattern was for Hindus, Muslims, and Sikhs to live side by side reasonably comfortably, especially in small villages. There, communities often had to share resources and abilities because survival depended on it.

The communal violence that attended partition can be traced to certain aspects of Indian history and village culture, as well as the circumstances of partition itself. First, Great Britain had used a policy of divide and rule in its Indian possessions. After the so-called mutiny of 1857, when Hindu and Muslim soldiers in Britain's Indian armies rose up against their officers and against British rule in principle, the British purposefully encouraged separation among Hindus, Muslims, and Sikhs. Leaders believed that by dividing the communities, order could be maintained and, more important, another large-scale rebellion could be prevented.[75]

Knowingly or not, Indian independence leaders picked up on the practice of divide and rule. Mahatma Gandhi's actions and sentiments were based in Hinduism despite his belief in the truth and equality of all religions, and many Indian Muslims scoffed at his argument that they did not constitute a true "nation" but were mostly Hindus who had converted and were therefore fundamentally Indian. Ironically, Gandhi also displeased Hindu fundamentalists. They found him far too open-minded with regard not only to Islam but also caste restrictions and the status of untouchables. After the government reforms of 1937, meanwhile, Hindu Congress members who found themselves in important positions often gave precedence to Hindus over Muslims. Muslim League leader Muhammad Ali Jinnah, for his part, stirred up Muslim communal feeling after 1937 with his claims that the British Raj would be replaced by a Hindu one.

The other trend was a shift in everyday relations among Hindus, Muslims, and Sikhs from 1942 on. The imminence of partition and the encouraging of communal conflict by leaders brought to the surface tensions often ignored or tolerated in the past. In villages, for instance, Muslims were often indebted to moneylenders for seed, fertilizer, and other resources. Since Muslims were forbidden by their religion to engage in money lending, their creditors were invariably Hindus. After the borders were announced in August 1947, Muslim farmers suddenly found it possible to free themselves from debt by forcing the moneylenders to flee to India or by simply killing them. Sikhs, meanwhile, remembered that it was Muslims who had targeted many of their seventeenth-century founders and plotted revenge for these long-ago acts, even though in earlier years few had worried overtly about such distant matters. On an even more trivial level, aspects of life and religion that in other times were little more than objects of curiosity or discussion—dietary prohibitions, dress, festivals—now became reasons to think of others as dangerous and threatening.

Greed also played a part in the partition riots. On both sides of the border, people saw opportunities to seize the property of those leaving. To encourage quick departures, looters and thieves threatened or carried out violent acts. Meanwhile, refugees themselves could be targeted by thieves in search of gold, jewelry, cash, and other portable valuables. Often, robbery turned into rape and murder. In some instances, attacks were carried out by organized bands, such as the Sikh *jathas*, often made up of former soldiers who had been recently demobilized.[76] The Sikhs, especially, were afraid that their very way of life was being threatened and were stirred up by radical leaders such as Tara Singh.

The cycle of violence spun out of control, and neither British, Indian, nor Pakistani authorities were able to do much about it until the riots had burned themselves out. Attacks inspired other attacks, as Hindus, Muslims, and Sikhs vowed revenge for atrocities committed by their enemies. Many found violence an outlet for their frustration and despair over having to leave homelands that, in many cases, their ancestors had lived in and cultivated for centuries.

There had already been small incidents, but the violence of partition truly began on August 16, 1946, the Muslim League's Direct Action Day. For that day Jinnah and the central working committee of the League had called for a "universal Muslim *hartal*" in response to what they saw as British duplicity and an egregious power grab by Congress in setting up an interim government the previous month. A hartal was a distinctly Indian form of protest, used often by the independence movement. It called for a complete stoppage of work, school, and other everyday activities. Hartals were supposed to be nonviolent and, in most of India, this one was, too. The major exception was Calcutta, India's most violent city and a place called the "city of dreadful night" by Rudyard Kipling, the British imperialist author. There, from August 16 to August 19, communal rioting left about 5,000 people dead and 15,000 more injured. Tens of thousands more were turned into exiles or refugees. Officials gradually restored order, but the poorer quarters of Calcutta remained in a constant state of tension and insecurity.[77]

The "Great Calcutta Killings" started a pattern that was to be repeated for many months. Calcutta Muslims had used the occasion of the hartal to target local Hindus and Sikhs. The latter groups then sought retaliation against Muslims. When, on September 2, the Congress-dominated interim government took office, a new wave of riots broke out in Bombay and other cities as Muslim activists turned the day into one of mourning. Attacks in Calcutta continued, and they indicate fairly clearly the back-and-forth nature of the communal killings. During September, 162 Muslims and 158 Hindus were killed there.[78]

The British viceroy, Lord Wavell, feared a complete collapse in public order and grew increasingly pessimistic about India's future. He seemed to take to heart Gandhi's warning that "if India wants her blood bath, she shall have it." Muslim League representatives were eventually brought into the interim government, which quelled the violence for a while, but Wavell was not reassured. He told the British cabinet toward the end of the year that he did not believe that the colonial government or its armed forces could hold India for another 18 months, as Prime Minister Attlee hoped. He had also been drawing up plans for the evacuation of British personnel in the event of a large-scale outbreak of violence. Wavell's attitude left Indian leaders in a troublesome position; it seemed the British could do little about the spread of violence but, because the Indians did not control the country yet, they could do little, either.

The next large-scale outbreak of violence occurred in the Noakhali and Tippera districts of eastern Bengal. It was a region with a long history of communal tension because of the large gap in wealth between Muslim peasant farmers and Hindu landlords and professionals. In a wave of attacks orchestrated, apparently, by a powerful Muslim League official who used both hired thugs and elements of the League's paramilitary wing, the Muslim National Guard, Noakhali erupted in a series of thefts, rapes, forced conversions, and murders.[79] Thousands of Hindu refugees fled westward to Calcutta and the province of Bihar, a bit farther west, bringing with them their stories of horror.[80]

In a continuation of the increasingly familiar pattern, Hindus responded to Noakhali with attacks on Bihari Muslims, and the violence even spread to Uttar Pradesh, the province to the west. In the Bihari case, the radical Hindu paramilitary group, the RSS (*Rashtriya Swayamsevak Sangh*, or National Personal Service Society), sometimes took part. In the last weeks of 1946, Hindu groups killed about 7,000 Bihari Muslims, an estimated 75 percent of whom were women and children.[81] A horrified Jawarharlal Nehru, the head of the interim government, nearly resigned in despair at the news of Noakhali and Bihar.

Mahatma Gandhi, unhappy with India's partition and distressed by the turn to violence, adopted the restoration of peaceful Hindu-Muslim relations as a personal crusade. He traveled to Noakhali in the aftermath of the violence there, and walked from village to village, visiting hundreds of Muslim and Hindu families and often asking from them something to eat and a place to sleep. Along the way, he begged these ordinary people to end any support for radical activists, and he tried to convince community leaders to sit down with one another and make their peace. He later visited Bihar, where he announced that "the sins of the Noakhali Muslims and of the Bihar Hindus are of the same magnitude and are equally condemnable."[82] Although Gandhi was usually received peacefully by villagers, he suffered occasional abuse from Muslims and from Hindu radicals.[83]

Vast outbreaks of rioting in the Punjab formed part of the context in which the Congress Party, the Muslim League, and British leaders devised their partition plan in the spring of 1947. By the time Lord Louis Mountbatten arrived to replace Wavell as viceroy and use his personal drive and charisma to move the process forward, the Punjab had erupted. The coalition government in the province, representing Hindus, Sikhs, and Muslims not affiliated with the Muslim League, was dissolved in March. This created an opening for radical Sikh separatists, who, led by Tara Singh, hoped to carve out their own independent state out

MAHATMA GANDHI: A "ONE-MAN BOUNDARY FORCE"

As the Punjab exploded into violence in the months before and after partition, many feared that the city of Calcutta would erupt as well. India's most violent city, Calcutta had been the center of the first major outbreak of partition riots, the "Great Calcutta Killings" of August 1946, which had left about 5,000 people dead.

In 1947, however, Calcutta remained mostly peaceful. The main reason was the presence of Mahatma Gandhi, the spiritual leader of India's independence movement and a man willing to risk his own life to preserve peace in India. In the decades following the World War I era (1914–1918), Gandhi had staged actions ranging from mass marches to hunger strikes to daily prayer meetings to move India toward independence. Also, as an advocate of nonviolence, he was horrified at the partition riots. In a manner keeping with his patterns of public action, he went to Calcutta in August 1947 to stage a hunger strike to keep the peace. On the tensest day, August 15, the day of independence, he was joined by Shaheed Suhrawardy, the leader of Calcutta's Muslims and the sort of corrupt politician whom Gandhi disliked. That day, peace held in Calcutta, and the two gave up their hunger strike. Lord Mountbatten, Britain's last leader of India, called Gandhi a "one-man boundary force." It was a reference to the other, official boundary force, a unit of 55,000 troops that was, even then, failing to maintain order in the Punjab.

Over the following weeks, as the Punjab erupted even more violently, Gandhi stayed in Calcutta, which remained peaceful. Every day, hundreds of thousands of Calcuttans—Hindu, Muslim, and Sikh—gathered in the city's central open space, the maidan, to try to catch a glimpse of the Mahatma as he went to his daily prayer meetings. By early September, several incidents and misunderstandings had brought communal violence to Calcutta. To stop it, Gandhi now proclaimed a "fast unto death." After more than three days of eating nothing, the Mahatma received a pledge from Calcutta's Hindu, Muslim, and Sikh leaders promising to stop any further communal violence. He ended his fast, and the communal leaders were true to their word. Calcutta's peace held.

In the spring of 1947, large-scale riots occurred in the Punjab region of India after the coalition government was disbanded. India's viceroy, Louis Mountbatten, is pictured here with his wife, Lady Edwina Mountbatten, inspecting the village of Kahuta, where 1,000 homes were destroyed in March of that year during the unrest.

of the Punjab. With Tara Singh calling for blood, Sikh activists attacked Muslim League representatives in Lahore, Amritsar, and other Punjabi cities and towns.[84] Muslims reacted in kind, and the riots, murders, robberies, and rapes spread from the towns to the countryside. Hindus were inevitably caught up in the violence. An incident there illustrates how small problems became the inspiration for large-scale communal violence. Soon after Mountbatten took office, he received a message from the British governor of the Punjab citing a small, domestic spat outside of the city of Rawalpindi: "A Muslim's water buffalo had wandered on to the property of his Sikh neighbor. When its owner sought to reclaim it, a fight, then a riot, erupted. Two hours later, a hundred human beings lay in the surrounding fields, hacked to death with scythes and knives because of the vagrant humours of a water buffalo."[85]

At the end of July 1947, Mountbatten took steps to form a Punjab Boundary Force to try to restore order to the region. It was to be led by a British officer but be mostly composed of Indian troops, many of them Nepali Buddhist Gurkhas, rather than Hindus, Muslims, or Sikhs. Numbering 55,000 altogether, the force would be advised by both Indian and Pakistani authorities both before and after independence.[86] Although the force hastily took the field, it could do little. There were simply not enough troops to cover the territory, a problem that was compounded by the fact that most of the violence was taking place in the countryside rather than the cities. In addition, the force could count on little local cooperation. Even the police, who generally came from the regions they patrolled, often took part in or ignored the communal violence.

The Punjab was still in flames when independence arrived. One British official wrote: "The Punjab is an absolute inferno and it is still going strong. Thousands have been murdered and tens and hundreds of thousands of refugees are streaming about. There has been a lot of arson. It will take generations of work to put things straight."[87] Mountbatten remembered looking down in despair from his airplane at the fires burning in towns and villages as he returned from the independence celebrations at Karachi to those in Delhi on August 13.[88] On August 14, Nehru heard from associates that in Lahore, a city he loved, fires were burning, and women and children seeking water were cut down by Muslim mobs. He said, "How am I going to talk tonight? How am I going to pretend there's joy in my heart for India's independence when I know Lahore, our beautiful Lahore, is burning?"[89] A British soldier on the scene spoke much more directly. He remembered that in parts of Lahore,

> Corpses lay in the gutter. Nearby a posse of Muslim police chatted unconcerned. A British major . . . had also arrived. He and his driver were collecting the bodies. Some were dead.

Some were dying. All were horribly mutilated. They were Sikhs. Their long hair and beards were matted with blood. An old man, not so bad as the rest, asked me where we were taking them. "To hospital," I replied, adding to hearten him, "You're not going to die."

"I shall," he said, "if there is a Muslim doctor."[90]

The violence in the Punjab was at its worst that August and September when, with the borders known, the great migrations began. Millions set out, carrying whatever they could. There were caravans of refugees miles long, with one containing an estimated 800,000 people leaving West Punjab for India.[91] The numbers could provide protection against attackers but not from shortages of food and water, nor from disease, and refugees suffered greatly.

Among the grimmest episodes of violence were those on the trains that traversed the region, especially those that traveled the short distance between Lahore and Amritsar. For refugees, trains were far quicker than walking, especially given the heat and the shortages of fresh food and water, but each train was overcrowded. For attackers, however, it was easy to judge who was on the trains simply by the direction they were traveling. They learned to stop the trains, sometimes with as simple a measure as placing a cow on the tracks. Then they would rob, rape, and murder with impunity. It was common for trains full of corpses to reach the stations in Lahore and Amritsar, as well as those of smaller towns. During these deadly weeks, "there were periods of four or five days at a stretch during which not a single train reached Lahore or Amritsar without its complement of dead and wounded."[92] An Indian army officer, K. P. Candeth, recalled, "I remember seeing a train come in from Pakistan and there wasn't a single live person on it; there were just bodies, dead and butchered. Now, that train entered India and the people saw it. And the next Pakistan-bound train that came, they set upon it, and the slaughter was terrible."[93] These "ghost trains," in the words of novelist Khushwant Singh in his story of the period, *Train to Pakistan*, have become part of the common memory of the era of partition.

As fall turned to winter, the violence wound down, even in the Punjab and in Delhi itself, now a city crowded with angry and hungry refugees. Nehru and Home Minister Vallabhbhai Patel convinced Mountbatten, now serving as India's governor-general, to head an emergency committee designed to restore order in the Punjab, while Indian leaders undertook the same effort in Delhi. Edwina Mountbatten took a leading role in refugee relief efforts and, as peace returned, some emphasized the blessing that, outside of the Punjab, both India and Pakistan had remained mostly peaceful.

The violence of partition had mostly burned itself out when, in early January 1948, Mahatma Gandhi settled in at Birla House in Delhi, the home of a wealthy industrialist who contributed much to the Mahatma's causes. He started another hunger strike there on January 12, demanding not only the end of communal violence but complete peace between India and Pakistan. This fast brought him near death, but he ended it when a settlement was negotiated between India and Pakistan; its main feature was an agreement by the Indian government to pay Pakistan forty million pounds that the Pakistanis claimed was theirs by right from the partition settlement.

On January 30, on the grounds of Birla House, Gandhi was on his way to his daily prayer meeting when he was assassinated by a Hindu fundamentalist named Nathuram Godse. Alerted, Mountbatten quickly reached the scene. Like all other leaders, he was afraid that the event would spark a new and even more brutal wave of violence, especially if a Muslim had pulled the trigger. As he entered the grounds of Birla House, and in response to a voice claiming that a Muslim had shot Gandhi, Mountbatten shouted, without knowing whether it was true: "You fool! Don't you know it was a Hindu?"[94]

Gandhi's death was a turning point. According to journalists Mark Tully and Zareer Masani, "more than any other event, Gandhi's death purged the country of communal hatred."[95]

Nevertheless, memories of the violence were long lasting and bitter, and they further separated two nations already divided by artificial borders. In future years, the two new nations were to carve out separate and often conflicting paths.

8

India after
the Partition

In 1991, during an era of revived communal tensions, India's newly elected prime minister, Narasimha Rao, proclaimed that "the only way to exist in India is to co-exist."[96] In the years since partition, India has had remarkable success in maintaining the unity of an extremely diverse population. Communal and ethnic tensions among the nation's different religious, linguistic, and cultural groups continue to exist, and these tensions have sometimes exploded into violence. Some of the most extreme communal movements have cited the Pakistani example, claiming that if Indian Muslims are a "nation" deserving of their own national state, then so, too, is their group, whether it be Sikhs or Tamils. Nevertheless, many Indians continue to hold to Rao's ideal of "coexistence" rather than the alternative that some fear (and a few hope for): fragmentation and the drawing of new arbitrary boundaries.

India has grown to become the world's largest democracy, and the nation has thrived despite many challenges. Once the upheaval of partition had calmed, and after Mahatma Gandhi's death had brought an end to the independence era, India's leaders set about creating this durable democratic system. Jawaharlal Nehru took the office of prime minister, where he served until his death in 1964. He remained both the public face and private conscience of India's democracy, and he became a renowned figure around the globe. Vallabhbai Patel, who "epitomized peasant India's durability and native shrewdness," was named deputy prime minister.[97] Patel's death in 1950, however, left India without a figure who could hope to match Nehru's stature, thus leaving "panditji," as Nehru was known in an honorific title implying both great respect and great affection, without any true rivals or even, as it happened, a clear successor.

Indian leaders' first major task was to write a constitution, and in the atmosphere of peace and toleration that prevailed after independence, it was Dr. B. R. Ambedkar, the leader of India's untouchables, who was chosen to chair the committee that created the document. When it became law in January 1950, India's constitution declared the country to be a "Sovereign

Democratic Republic and Union of States." With Nehru's insistence, all adults were granted the right to vote regardless of educational level or property ownership. The constitution also
granted a full menu of personal liberties and allowed for protec-
tions for the nation's minorities or traditionally oppressed
groups.[98]

India has a president, but as with in many democracies,
India's president holds a largely ceremonial post. The true head
of the government is the prime minister, who presides over the
Lok Sabha, or "House of the People," India's equivalent to the
British House of Commons. Most of India's prime ministers
have been heads of the Congress Party, which dominated Indian
politics until the 1990s. The nation's upper house is known as
the Rajya Sabha, or "Assembly of States," and it holds less practical authority than the Lok Sabha.[99]

One way in which modern India has managed its regional-
ism and diversity is by employing a loose federal structure in
which the nation is divided into states that enjoy a good degree
of autonomy. As the nation has evolved, however, the nature
and number of these states has changed. At first, Indian leaders
inherited the provinces of British India and added to them the
former princely states. In the 1950s, though, Nehru came to
realize that linguistic borders in many ways made the most
sense, especially after the majority of Indians refused to accept
Hindi, the major language of northern India, as the national
tongue.[100] Today, there are 18 official Indian languages (and
hundreds of smaller languages and dialects). India's states
include Tamil Nadu in the south, where Tamil language and
culture predominate; Maharashtra along the central west coast,
which contains the city of Bombay (now Mumbai) and where
Marathi is the major language; and West Bengal, where Bengali
is spoken. In most of the states of northern India, including
Uttar Pradesh, the largest, Hindi is spoken, but others throughout the country have their own language. This linguistic clamor,
a sign of not only the persistence but the strengthening of earlier boundaries, has helped to ensure that English, ironically,

remains the nation's common tongue. Meanwhile, many of the states have followed very distinct paths politically; for many years West Bengal had an elected communist government, as did the southern state of Kerala. Kerala also has India's highest literacy rate, which can be attributed to its generous educational policies.

Despite India's vibrant and complex democracy, it has been dominated, at the top, by a political dynasty: the Nehrus. After Jawaharlal Nehru died in 1964, his daughter, Indira Gandhi, rose to prominence within the Congress Party and, after a brief interlude where an old party intellectual, Lal Bahadur Shastri, served as prime minister, she was elected in her own right in 1966. (Indira was no relation to Mahatma Gandhi; she was married to Feroze Gandhi.) Indira remained in power until 1977, presiding over agricultural reforms that helped make the nation self-sufficient, as well as overseeing India's first "peaceful" nuclear explosion in 1974.[101]

Fearful of political opposition, Indira declared an "emergency" in 1975. This emergency was a major challenge to India's democracy, as the prime minister used it to suspend normal democratic procedures and such liberties as the freedom of the press. She also placed many rival politicians, including famed figures from the independence era such as Morarji Desai, in prison. Some Indians feared that Indira's emergency might turn India into a true hereditary dynasty because of the power and influence wielded by her unelected son, Sanjay Gandhi. Among the programs in which Sanjay was heavily involved in these years was the state birth-control effort; designed to slow India's rapid population growth. It featured not only the aggressive promotion of various birth-control methods but also forced sterilizations, which were often organized and carried out by corrupt government officials seeking to curry favor with superiors.[102] Sanjay was also connected to slum clearance programs in cities, which often had the effect of forcing people to live on the streets rather than improving their housing.

Indira called for elections in 1977 and was ousted by a

Indira Gandhi, the daughter of India's first prime minister, Jawaharlal Nehru, was elected prime minister in 1966. Gandhi is pictured here in 1973 with her sons, Rajiv (to her immediate right) and Sanjay, daughter-in-law, Sonia, and grandchildren Priyanki and Rahul. Rajiv later served as prime minister after his mother was assassinated in 1984.

populace tired of the extremism that had emerged. The new prime minister was Morarji Desai, but he was unable to control India's factions, and Indira returned to office in 1980. Later that year, Sanjay Gandhi died when the plane that he was piloting crashed over Delhi. His elder brother, Rajiv, Indira's only other child, was elected to the Lok Sabha in his place. Rajiv, an Indian Airlines pilot with an Italian-born wife, Sonia, had little interest in politics. But his family loyalty trumped other concerns, as did his popularity with young members of the branch of the now-split Congress Party, and he duly took office.

Both Indira and Rajiv suffered greatly from a revival, in the

1980s and 1990s, of India's communal conflicts. In October 1984, Indira was assassinated by Sikh members of her bodyguard. The Sikhs were reacting to what many in their community saw as

OPERATION BLUE STAR AND ITS AFTERMATH

In the early 1980s, India faced a militant separatist movement among the Sikhs in the Punjab. The movement was a sign that India was still divided by arbitrary borders of religion and culture and that some of its peoples thought of themselves as separate nations, just as the Muslims had claimed in the years leading up to partition. The leader of the Sikh militants, Sant Jarnail Singh Bhindranwale, demanded that the Sikhs be granted their own state, Khalistan. He incited communal tensions by claiming that the Sikhs were being oppressed by Hindus. Meanwhile, some of his followers had infiltrated the police and local governments in areas across the Punjab, making it a lawless and dangerous place.

By mid-1984, Bhindranwale and a number of armed followers were holed up in the Golden Temple in the city of Amritsar, the Sikh's holiest site, and they pledged to remain there until an independent Khalistan was created. The Indian government under Indira Gandhi, which rejected any thought of separatism and deplored the lawlessness of the Punjab, surrounded the Golden Temple with army troops on June 2, in what was known as Operation Blue Star. On June 5, the army entered the temple grounds. The result was a major battle that left hundreds of troops and even more civilians dead or wounded. The fighting also destroyed parts of the Golden Temple itself, as well as many important Sikh documents and relics. Although Operation Blue Star ended the immediate threat from Bhindranwale, who was killed in the fighting, it also left Sikhs across India embittered.

On October 31, Indira Gandhi, who had been India's prime minister for most of the previous 20 years, was assassinated by two members of her Sikh bodyguard. She had rejected calls to maintain bodyguards only from other communities, claiming that she could not be afraid of any Indian. Her assassination further enflamed the troubled relations between Sikhs and Hindus. Over the days that followed, 1,000 Sikhs were killed in riots in Delhi alone, as India suffered its worst communal violence since the aftermath of partition. Sikhs responded with similar attacks, and the Punjab remained dangerous for many more years.

excessively violent government repression of a Sikh separatist movement in the Punjab. By acclamation, Rajiv Gandhi, at the age of 40, was sworn in as India's new prime minister on October 31, 1984, the day of his mother's assassination.

Sikh terrorism continued for many more years, but Rajiv found he had another major instance of communal trouble to contend with as well. In the south, some Tamils were actively supporting the violent revolutionary movement of their cultural counterparts in Sri Lanka. Some of these Sri Lankan "Tamil Tigers" wanted to unite the island with Tamil Nadu in a new country, although most wanted only an autonomous Tamil-speaking state on the island itself. To help maintain the peace in Sri Lanka and lessen the tension in Tamil Nadu, Rajiv sent in the Indian Army in 1987. While running for reelection in 1991 after having been ousted in 1989, Rajiv was killed by a bomb set by a Tamil Tiger.[103]

The Nehru dynasty was not yet at an end. After Rajiv's assassination, calls came from some members of Congress for his wife, the Italian-born Sonia, to step into his place. Initially she refused, but the power of the Nehru and Gandhi names, and the unity and hope they represented, remained powerful. Sonia finally agreed to serve at the head of the Congress-I Party (the result of the earlier split—the "I" is for Indira) in 1998. Congress-I was able to return a government to the Lok Sabha in 2004, although Sonia refused to serve as prime minister. She remains, despite her Italian heritage, a figure of reverence among many ordinary Indians, and her son, Rahul, ran successfully for a seat in the Lok Sabha in 2004.[104]

Communal tensions among Hindus and Muslims also reappeared in the 1990s, although they had never truly died away. India's Muslim population remains substantial at well over 100 million. Many of them have felt like members of an oppressed minority despite the guarantees of their equality in India's constitution; some complained that Indira's policies of forced sterilizations and slum clearance were disproportionately aimed at Muslims.[105]

Some Hindus, on the other hand, feel that their traditions are under threat, not necessarily from Muslims, who number less than 15 percent of the population, but from modern India's secular nature. Traditionalists argue that India's government has protected its minorities at the expense of the Hindu majority—that it has "coddled" Muslims and members of other minority groups who refuse to accept the essential *Hindutva* or "Hinduness" of India, a conception that Nehru and other founders would have rejected. One activist group of Hindu traditionalists, the Shiv Sena Party of Maharashtra, has asserted that Muslims in India must accept, in effect, subordinate status as members of a minority.[106] On a nationwide scale, the Bharatiya Janata Party (BJP) rose to prominence in the late 1980s on a platform of defending the interests of Hindu traditionalists.

These parties are concerned with not only the protected status of Muslims but also that of low-caste Hindus and untouchables. In the 1950s, Indian leaders tried to end longstanding arbitrary social boundaries by banning discrimination based on caste, and Dr. Ambedkar's *Dalit* Party of untouchables rose to become one of India's largest. Leaders went on to enact measures preserving certain privileges for low-caste Hindus and untouchables, such as receiving a percentage of civil service jobs and being admitted to universities. When these privileges were confirmed by the Mandal Commission (in the 1990s), upper-caste Hindus rioted in Delhi in protest, fearful of losing their traditional position among India's elite, which they had held even under British rule.[107] Nehru's insistence on universal suffrage, however, has prevented any anti-low caste or untouchable movement from growing too widespread; these groups simply make up too large a majority of India's voting population and wield a great deal of power in state governments. When the BJP took power in the late 1990s, under Prime Minister Atal Bihari Vajpayee, it was forced to tone down its rhetoric and engage in compromises.

The relatively recent rise of Hindu traditionalism, or fundamentalism, as some call it, has resulted in India's most recent major outbreak of Hindu-Muslim communal violence. In 1990,

Hindu traditionalists called for the tearing down of the Babri Masjid Mosque in the city of Ayodha. The mosque had been constructed by the sixteenth-century Mughal emperor Babur on the site of a previous Hindu temple that honored the alleged birthplace of the god Rama, hero of the epic, the Ramayana. Certain Hindus demanded that this "historical injustice" be corrected and the site once again dedicated to Rama. Tensions finally exploded in December 1992 when "a mob of frenzied Hindu fanatics shouting 'Ram, Ram' . . . reduced Babri Masjid to rubble and choking dust, while Indian soldiers and police watched in smiling approval."[108] A nationwide outbreak of rioting followed, but it was at its most intense in Bombay, where Hindu and Muslim mobs engaged in murder, looting, and burning in ways reminiscent of the partition riots of 1946 and 1947. The violence even spilled over into Pakistan and Bangladesh, where rioters attacked Hindu temples, signaling that on their sides of the borders, too, the memories of India's arbitrary partition remained very much alive.

One of independent India's greatest issues has been extreme poverty; the boundaries between rich and poor are perhaps the nation's most troubling problem. It is also likely that wealth disparities have contributed to the reappearance of conflict between Hindus and Muslims.[109] Jawaharlal Nehru believed that the most likely cure for this chronic poverty was an economy organized on socialist lines, with state control of certain industries. State-designed financing for heavy industry, such as coal and steel, would be instituted, and barriers to foreign trade and investment such as tariffs, the latter intended to encourage local industries to produce goods for domestic consumption rather than to allow India to be overrun by foreign imports as it was during British times, would be put into place.[110] By the 1980s, however, Nehru's approach, which was largely maintained by his successors, had begun to frustrate many Indians who saw a world moving toward less direct government involvement in industry, as well as freer international trade.

Economic reforms authored in the early 1990s by Manmohan

Singh—who in 2004 became India's first Sikh prime minister in a sure sign that the nation's cultural borders are never absolute—opened up India to foreign investment and greater competition, and the nation's entrepreneurial population responded enthusiastically, providing the country with one of the fastest-growing economies on Earth. The southern city of Bangalore has emerged as India's "silicon plain" and is now a global center of high-tech development, whereas the nation's film industry, known as "Bollywood" because it is based in Bombay, is the world's largest. Bombay itself, meanwhile, is India's financial center, with real estate values rivaling those of New York City, London, or Tokyo. With trade barriers lowered, it is now possible to buy in India such international brands as Coca-Cola®, rather than be restricted to India's locally made substitutes, Thums-up or Campa. A global population of nonresident Indians, or NRIs, has contributed its savings and expertise to India's growth, as well—one of the nation's great advantages has been its large population of well-educated, English-speaking, and by the standards of Western Europe or the United States, inexpensive workers. At nearly 150 million people, India now has the largest middle class of any country in the world, partially balancing the millions who remain extremely poor in the country's thousands of rural villages, as well as the slums and shantytowns of big cities.[111]

In foreign policy, India's greatest challenge has always been Pakistan. Aside from a brief and indecisive war with China over disputed border regions in India's far north in 1964 and "peacekeeping" efforts in Sri Lanka in the 1980s, the nation's wars have all been with Pakistan. The first was in late 1947, over the still-troubled province of Kashmir. The second took place in 1965. It started with disputes over military activity along Pakistan's southern border with India, then spread north to include the Punjab and Kashmir as well. Like the first war, this one was settled with a United Nations cease-fire, but only after Indian tanks and troops had crossed the border and reached the outskirts of the major Pakistani city of Lahore. The third war, in 1971, resulted in a decisive victory for India's military forces and split East Pakistan from West Pakistan. The result was a new nation: Bangladesh. Arbitrary borders had sundered the subcontinent once again.

Tensions between India and Pakistan remain high. In Kashmir in particular, there are frequent incidents such as bombings and kidnappings, and both countries maintain a strong military presence in their portions of the disputed province. This ongoing problem has become even more urgent in recent years. By the spring of 1998, both India and Pakistan became official nuclear powers, possessing the capability of both building and then delivering nuclear weapons.

India's status as an official nuclear power, and its size and strategic position in South Asia, assure the nation's continued geopolitical importance, and it is quite possible that India will be granted a permanent seat on the United Nations Security Council once that body engages in major reforms. It will likely have much to contribute. Almost from the beginning, Indian leaders carved out their own path in foreign policy. Nehru was among the founders of the so-called nonaligned movement— nations that during the cold war sided neither with the democratic West nor the communist Soviet Union. Nehru and his successors, notably Indira Gandhi, also sought to develop meaningful cultural and economic ties with the Soviet Union, which sometimes led to charges by Western powers that India was "soft on communism" and led them, the United States in particular, to support Pakistan as a result.

Despite outbreaks of violence and discord, and despite still-chronic poverty, seemingly unstoppable population growth, and a bureaucracy mired in corruption and inertia, India's democracy has indeed thrived and the nation has held together. Historian Stanley Wolpert has written that "India's unique linguistic and ethnic pluralism make that nation more vulnerable to . . . fragmenting demands than virtually any other state in the world."[112] Yet the nation's democratic leaders, most of the time following Jawaharlal Nehru's line of secularism, tolerance, and the rule of law, have managed not only to check these "fragmenting demands" but also to strengthen the country.

They had a strong legacy on which to build. In response to those who in the wake of the Sikhs' Khalistan movement, the activities of the Tamil Tigers, the Babri Masjid riots, and other separatist and communal movements predicted that India was likely to fall apart, author and former United Nations official Shashi Taroor wrote: "India is a country held together, in Nehru's evocative image, by strong but invisible threads that bind Indians to a common destiny. Indians are comfortable with multiple identities and multiple loyalties, all coming together in an allegiance to a larger idea of India, an India that safeguards the common space available to each identity; an India that remains safe for diversity."[113] These "strong but invisible threads" are the legacy of the idea of India that held the region together during centuries of foreign rule and help to make modern India, despite the arbitrary borders created in 1947, the inheritor of the subcontinent's thousands of years of continuity.

9

Pakistan after the Partition

On September 1, 1948, Muhammad Ali Jinnah died of cancer. Just a little more than a year earlier, Pakistan, the nation that Jinnah had devoted the last years of his life to creating, celebrated its independence. Fittingly, Jinnah had served as the nation's first governor-general, continuing in the role of the Quaid-i-Azam, or "great leader," of India's Muslims that he had held for years, even though as a Westernized figure who smoke and drank and rarely observed prayers or other services, Jinnah was an indifferent Muslim.

Jinnah's successor as the leader of Pakistan, already holding the office of prime minister, was Liaquat Ali Khan, who had served as Jinnah's chief lieutenant in Pakistan's independence negotiations. Like Jinnah, Liaquat Ali was a Westernized, secular figure. Unhappy with that, and also frustrated by the prime minister's failure to act aggressively with regard to the issue of Kashmir, a small group of conspirators arranged to have Liaquat Ali assassinated in October 1951. Subsequently, "Pakistan fell under the control, first, of a series of pedestrian civil bureaucrats reared in British service traditions and, after 1958, under the steel frame of martial 'law.'"[114]

Pakistan's first years of independence, therefore, were quite different from those in neighboring India, where the presence of Jawaharlal Nehru and the government's status as the inheritor of the subcontinent's many traditions provided a large measure of political stability and continuity. Pakistan, instead, had to create a nation almost from scratch. Unlike in India, there was no particular logic to Pakistan, a problem that was exacerbated by the fact that the country was divided into two "wings": West Pakistan was carved from the former British Indian provinces of Sind and Baluchistan (from the Northwest Frontier Province) and parts of the Punjab and Kashmir. It contained the nation's first capital, Karachi, as well as most of its major military installations. East Pakistan, the other "wing," was made up mostly of the eastern portion of Bengal province. Its population, which was larger than that of the western wing, had a vastly different culture from that of West Pakistan and maintained separatist sentiments of its own. Further, West Pakistani politicians hesitated to weaken their power by granting the easterners the representation in the national government that their population justified. Beyond these considerations was the fact that Pakistan had effectively seceded from a much larger and longer-lasting entity, India. To novelist Salman Rushdie, who traces his heritage back to both countries, "to build Pakistan it was necessary to cover up Indian history, to deny that Indian centuries lay just beneath the surface."[115] This building process continues.

The commander-in-chief of Pakistan's army, Mohammad Ayub Khan, seized political control in 1958, and the nation's subsequent history was one of military coups and countercoups punctuated by occasional, quasi-democratic elections. Early in Ayub Khan's rule, Pakistani leaders moved their capital from Karachi, which lay far away from the nation's other major population centers and military installations, to a new city, Islamabad. Ayub Khan's first major challenger was Fatima Jinnah, Muhammad Ali Jinnah's sister, who ran for president of Pakistan in 1964 but did not win because of Ayub Khan's limiting of the franchise in managed elections. His second opponent was an East Pakistani Bengali politician, Sheikh Mujibur Rahman, who emerged to prominence in 1966 as head of the so-called Awami League. Rahman called for greater autonomy for East Pakistan, including an independent military and a separate currency. His third opponent was Zulfikar Ali Bhutto, a sophisticated politician descended from a wealthy Sindhi family. Ali Bhutto had risen to prominence as a diplomat under Ayub Khan, but had since split with the leader. He formed the so-called Pakistani People's Party in 1967, pledging a sort of "Islamic socialism." In 1968, both Mujibur Rahman and Ali Bhutto were arrested, although far from halting Pakistan's apparent fragmentation, the arrests inspired civil unrest in both West and East Pakistan among the two leaders' supporters. Ayub Khan retired in 1969, turning power over to another general, Aga Muhammad Yahya Khan, who was willing to use greater force to limit public expressions of political discontent, especially in the east.

In December 1970, Pakistan held nationwide elections, the results of which showed that strong boundaries of cultural and political interests separated the nation's two wings. The two great victors were Mujibur Rahman, whose party nearly swept all the seats allotted to East Pakistan in the National Assembly in Pakistan's new capital of Islamabad, and Ali Bhutto, whose Pakistani People's Party took the majority of votes in the west. His decisive victory should have allowed Mujibur Rahman to become Pakistan's prime minister, but neither Ali Bhutto, now serving as deputy prime minister, nor Yahya Khan, were willing to accept a Bengali as the leader of Pakistan.[116] When the three

PAKISTAN SPLITS: THE WAR FOR BANGLADESH

One of the clearest of the arbitrary borders left in the wake of India's partition in 1947 was the separation between the eastern and western "wings" of the new nation of Pakistan. Even though the overwhelming majority of the inhabitants of both wings were Muslim, they had little else in common. The Punjabis, Sindhis, and Pathans of West Pakistan had completely different languages and cultural traditions than the Bengalis of East Pakistan. In fact, the easterners had greater affinity toward the Hindu Bengalis of Calcutta and the rest of Indian West Bengal.

In 1966, the politician Sheikh Mujibur Rahman, unhappy with the fact that his Bengali home of East Pakistan was often ignored by leaders in West Pakistan, produced a document that was to provide the foundation of an independent Bangladesh, a political partition of Pakistan that would echo the partition of India in 1947. His six-point program called for nearly full autonomy for East Pakistan; new electoral procedures; a separate East Pakistani militia; a separate currency; independent control over foreign earnings; and almost complete control over taxation in the province. Pakistan's government could not approve these demands, but when Rahman's party won nearly all of East Pakistan's assembly seats in 1970, he could no longer be ignored. After Rahman called for a general strike in East Pakistan, the nation's military leader, General Yahya Khan, sent a large force of 60,000 troops to the east to maintain order.

proved unable to come to an agreement, East Pakistan declared its independence as Bangladesh, and the Pakistani army failed to hold its recalcitrant eastern wing. The Indian Army stepped in, as Indian leaders were fearful of a massive wave of refugees crossing the border into Calcutta and the rest of Indian West Bengal, and the independence of Bangladesh came to fruition in December 1971.

As had been the case in Pakistan's early years, at first the new leaders of Bangladesh clung to a democratic ideal, but by 1974 Mujibur Rahman abandoned democratic processes in favor of a more powerful executive branch, citing excessive corruption and

In March 1971, brutal fighting broke out between these troops and the local people, who now demanded full independence and formed themselves into militias. Rahman was arrested and imprisoned, and millions of Bengalis fled across the border into India to escape the expanding violence. At the United Nations, India decried the bloodbath in East Pakistan and also grew concerned about how they were to feed and house millions of refugees crossing a Bengali border that had recently been created. The United States, for its part, sided with Pakistan, unhappy with India's flirtations with the Soviet Union. In October, a large, Indian-trained force of Bengalis moved back into East Pakistan to do battle with Yahya Khan's troops. They were followed by three divisions of the Indian army, supported by the air force. India and Pakistan were now fighting their third war since independence.

Pakistani aircraft attacked Indian cities in the west, and India responded with its much greater air-power capability, stifling any possible Pakistani advances. In the east, India's forces moved quickly on the local administrative capital of Dhaka, as Pakistan's troops, now holding out among a very hostile population, could not hope for any reinforcements. Pakistan surrendered on December 15, 1971, and the new nation of Bangladesh was born. Mujibur Rahman returned to Dhaka in triumph. The Indian subcontinent had once again been partitioned.

other internal threats to the nation. He was assassinated during a military coup in Dhaka, the nation's capital, in August 1975, and Bangladesh succumbed to a series of military dictatorships of varying degrees of effectiveness and severity for years. In recent years, Bangladesh has relied on legitimately elected leaders, but it remains subject to political violence and instability.

In Pakistan itself, Ali Bhutto rose to the pinnacle of leadership. After a strong denunciation during negotiations in the United Nations Security Council of India's interference in the war in East Pakistan, Bhutto returned to Pakistan to find that he had secured the backing of the nation's military and civil elite. During a nonviolent coup, General Yahya Khan was convinced to step aside, and Bhutto replaced him as prime minister. Under his leadership, Pakistani politicians devised and approved a new constitution, which took effect on August 14, 1973. It was Pakistan's third.[117] Among its major changes from previous constitutions was the declaration that "Islam shall be the state religion of Pakistan."[118] Muhammad Ali Jinnah, by contrast, had declared in 1947 that Pakistan was to have complete freedom of religion, that "religious caste or creed . . . has nothing to do with the state."[119]

In 1977, after elections had been deemed unsatisfactory by Ali Bhutto's opponents, the prime minister was forced from power by yet another military coup, this one led by General Muhammad Zia ul-Haq. Bhutto himself was imprisoned and, in April 1979, executed after being found guilty of conspiracy to engage in political murder in a mysterious incident in 1974.[120] After a reasonably peaceful period, during which Zia ul-Haq largely managed to maintain order as well as his own popularity, the general died in an airplane crash in August 1988. Among his strongest legacies was the increased presence of Islamic tradition in government, such as elements of *Sharia*, Islamic law as described in the Koran. Zia ul-Haq did not want to create a theocracy in Pakistan; his feelings were more sophisticated and subtle, although they still differed notably from those of Jinnah, the nation's founder. Zia ul-Haq argued in 1981 that "Pakistan is like Israel, an ideological state. Take out Judaism from Israel and it will collapse like a house of cards. Take Islam out of Pakistan and make it a secular state; it would collapse."[121] Sharia is open to varied interpretation, as Pakistan's politicians and legal experts were to discover. Despite Zia ul-Haq's views and the emergence of conservative Islamic political parties, though, most of Pakistan's elite cling to the notion that their nation should remain a secular one, where Muslims can live and worship free from oppression. Most Pakistanis have been "content to let Islam guide individual behavior rather than become the religion of the state."[122] In this, they seem to hold more to Jinnah's conception of Pakistan as a nation of people bound together by tradition and culture as well as religion, rather than Zia ul-Haq's notion of religious "ideology" alone.

This secular emphasis has helped Islamabad politicians hold together a nation containing a broad diversity of linguistic and ethnic groups. Since most of these groups are Muslim, there are fewer sources of religious tension than in neighboring India. Nevertheless, linguistic, economic, and cultural tensions still exist among these people, thrown together by the creation of arbitrary geographical borders. For example, although Urdu is the nation's main language, the tongue in which government business and most educational instruction are conducted, 48 percent of the population speaks Punjabi as their first language. Other major languages include Sindhi as well as Pashtun, one of the languages spoken by the many tribal groups who inhabit the frontier regions of Pakistan and Afghanistan. Some members of these groups advocate complete separation from Pakistan. Another outspoken and discontented group, the *Mujahirs*, is made up of migrants from India, many of them wealthy and with strong economic ties to India. Most have settled in Karachi and have little long-term personal identification with Pakistan.[123] Hindu or Sikh groups in Pakistan, meanwhile, are quite small and not organized in such a way as to allow meaningful communal action.

After a brief period of government under longtime president Ghulam Ishaq Khan following Zia's death in 1988, Ali Bhutto's

Benazir Bhutto, the first woman to head the government of a Muslim state, became prime minister of Pakistan in 1988. The daughter of former Pakistani prime minister Ali Bhutto, Benazir currently lives in exile in the United Arab Emirates.

daughter Benazir Bhutto became prime minister. Among her promises was to return Pakistan to status as a full democracy, and many Pakistanis were happy that a civilian government had now replaced the military one of the last 11 years. The pattern of factional squabbling, charges, and countercharges continued, however.[124] During the 1990s, Benazir Bhutto returned to power once, holding office from October 1993 to February 1997. Nawaz Sharif, her main opponent and the head of the Muslim League, held office both before and after her second term. Both presided over civilian, elected governments. Pakistan's political instability created a vacuum of authority in which the nation's elite, army, and traditional landlords especially, wielded a great deal of influence, however.[125] When Sharif made the decision to force aside his army chief of staff, General Pervez Musharraf, the general staged yet another of Pakistan's military coups. Musharraf took over Pakistan on October 12, 1999, and remains the nation's leader, with Sharif and Benazir Bhutto occasionally voicing vocal opposition.

Pakistan's political instability has shadowed the nation's role in international politics. Beginning in the 1950s, and partly in response to India's nonaligned status, Pakistan became a major ally of the United States during the Cold War. As such, Pakistan received a great deal of military and economic aid from the West. Being a recipient of military aid, in particular, may have given Pakistani leaders a false sense of the nation's military capabilities; it was only after their loss in the war over Bangladesh that Pakistani leaders stopped trying to be India's military equal. Then, after the Soviet Union invaded Afghanistan in 1979, Pakistan became a staging point for Western efforts to support anti-Soviet rebels in Afghanistan, bringing in more aid, much of which was designed to support the more than a million Afghan refugees who fled across the porous border between the two countries. During the 1980s, for instance, Pakistan was the "third largest recipient of American aid after Israel and Egypt," and it was described as a bulwark against the spread of communism.[126] In the new millennium, Pakistan found itself once again at the front line of international conflict, this time with the fight against Islamic fundamentalist terrorists based in Afghanistan. Pledging to support the United States and other nations in their attempts to control Afghanistan's Taliban fundamentalists and their global allies, the Islamabad government has once again been a recipient of foreign aid. One unforeseen consequence of this in contentious Pakistan has been the rise of Islamic fundamentalism in some segments of the populace, although the government, and the majority of the population, remains committed to secularism in public life.

Muhammad Ali Jinnah had worried, in the years and months leading up to independence, whether he might inherit a "moth-eaten Pakistan," shorn of the economic capabilities of West Bengal and the eastern Punjab, both of which were awarded to

India. As it happened, Pakistan proved very capable of supporting itself, at least until the 1990s, when many signs of trouble became apparent. In the 1980s, in fact, World Bank statistics suggested that Pakistan was on the verge of crossing a significant economic boundary: moving from the status of a low-income country to that of a middle-income one.[127] Certain areas of the country, especially the Punjab, remained strong in its agricultural production, and by the end of the 1980s, Pakistan was producing a substantial surplus of food grains, as well as cotton, much of which was sold to the Islamic Middle East. In industry, too, Pakistan held its own despite much government manipulation and corruption. By the 1990s, however, poverty was increasing, industry had reached a state of stagnation, and the nation's national debt was so extensive that Pakistan was nearly bankrupt.[128]

In May 1998, Pakistan staged its first public tests of nuclear weapons. Always a nation with a cohort of highly educated citizens, Pakistan had been theoretically capable of building nuclear weapons for years. Only after India publicly tested its own weapons did Pakistan respond with its tests, though, and both nations are now officially members of a select group of acknowledged nuclear powers. This has inspired increased tensions between the two nations, which, since partition, have gone to war three times. With nuclear capability comes a sense of responsibility, however, and leaders on both sides have made halting gestures that suggest that they understand they must live side by side—that they must come to terms with the arbitrary geographical borders of 1947.

Some of these gestures are fairly simple: For instance, after many years, it is now possible to travel by bus between the Indian city of Amritsar and the Pakistani city of Lahore. The two stand only 40 miles apart, and were the center of the violence that attended partition in 1947. In March 2004, the Indian national cricket team made its first ever tour of Pakistan; both nations love the sport, and matches between the two have sometimes looked like symbolic wars. The tour went peacefully,

Known as the "line of control (LOC)," the border that separates Indian Kashmir from Pakistani Kashmir has been a flashpoint since the early 1970s—more than 15,000 civilians have been killed over the years along the border. Indian army soldiers are pictured here near Akhnoor, India, patrolling the border between the two countries.

despite the fact that the Indian team defeated its Pakistani counterpart. Also, since 2003, summit meetings between Pervez Musharraf and his Indian counterparts Atal Bihari Vajpayee and Manmohan Singh created still more hopes for stronger ties between the two countries. The British Broadcasting Company reported on April 17, 2005, that people living in the border regions of the Punjab were preparing roadways and shops for greater cross-border travel and trade, even without official word from either government that controls would be further reduced and the borders opened. For many of them, the borderline has always been fairly arbitrary.

Recently, Pakistan and India have even been making progress

on the issue that divides them most: Kashmir. In 1972, the border that separated Indian Kashmir from Pakistan's portion was designated a "line of control (LOC)" pending future negotiations. Islamic militants and Kashmiri separatists have ensured that the region has remained unstable and dangerous, with some 15,000 civilians killed over the years. In 2002, India and Pakistan nearly came to war once again over violations of the LOC. Musharraf and Singh stated in April 2005, however, that they hoped to turn the LOC into a "soft border," across which it would be easier for people to move. One feature of this new "soft border" is bus service, which began in April 2005. The first cross-Kashmir bus trips were successful and peaceful—despite threats from militants—and Pakistani and Indian leaders entered into talks to add new cross-border services in the Punjab beginning in November 2005. And in the face of the massive death toll and destruction of an October 2005 earthquake, leaders agreed to open further border points to ease the flow of aid.

There is little chance that Pakistan and India will be reunited in the foreseeable future, or that the problem of Kashmir will be solved to the satisfaction of all sides. The far greater possibility is that, as has been so often the case in the history of the subcontinent, these borders will become increasingly irrelevant—that the arbitrary borders imposed in 1947 and after are, like all arbitrary borders, subject to change. If both Indians and Pakistanis are able to move across the borderline easily, and if goods and ideas flow just as easily, ordinary people on both sides of the border may yet move again toward a new version of the subcontinent's historical ideal of unity in diversity.

B.C.

2800–1800 The Indus Valley civilization, the first large-scale urban civilization in India, develops.

1500–500 Indo-Aryans migrate into India; the caste system emerges.

326–184 The Mauryan Dynasty controls North India and creates India's first imperial unification.

A.D.

320–550 The Gupta Dynasty controls North India.

711 The first Muslims settle in northwestern India.

850–1267 The Chola kingdom dominates South India.

997 Mahmud of Ghazni begins a long series of plundering raids into India from Afghanistan.

1206 The Delhi Sultanate is established.

1336–1565 The Hindu kingdom of Vijayanagar controls most of South India.

1526 Muslim conqueror Babur establishes the Mughal Empire.

1612 English traders build their first outpost.

1690 The English East India Company founds Calcutta.

1757 East India Company armies seize control of Bengal.

1857 The Sepoy Rebellion takes place.

1858 The British Crown takes direct control of India.

1885 The Indian National Congress is founded.

1905 The first (unsuccessful) partition of Bengal takes place.

1906 The Muslim League is founded.

1919 The Amritsar Massacre occurs.

1929 Jawaharlal Nehru becomes the president of the Congress Party; Indian independence leaders pledge to work for full independence.

1931 Mahatma Gandhi conducts his salt march; Muslim League representatives propose and name Pakistan.

1935 Britain proposes a Government of India Act.

1937 A revised Government of India Act allows for Indian politicians to run India's provinces; Muhammad Ali

Jinnah enlarges the Muslim League, so it can compete with Congress.

1939 Britain and India enter World War II.

1940 The Muslim League makes its Pakistan Resolution.

1942 A British mission led by Sir Stafford Cripps fails to make a satisfactory independence proposal; the Quit India movement results in most congressional leaders being imprisoned.

1943 Subhas Chandra Bose founds the Indian National Army.

1945 World War II ends; Labour leader Clement Attlee replaces Conservative Winston Churchill as British prime minister and pledges quick independence for India; elections establish the Muslim League as the

326 B.C.
The Mauryan Dynasty
takes control of North India

1526
The Mughal Empire
is established

1885
The Indian National Congress
begins the independence
movement

1940
The Muslim League
pledges to work for an
independent Pakistan

B.C. 326   1942

A.D. 997
Muslim warlord
Mahmud of
Ghazni begins
plundering raids
into India

1757
The British begin
to build their
Indian empire

1931
Mahatma Gandhi
conducts his
salt march

1942
The Quit India Movement
takes place

main representative of India's Muslims; Congress Party leaders refuse to accept the possibility of partition.

1946 Sir Stafford Cripps returns to devise independence plans satisfactory to both Congress and the Muslim League; INA officers are tried by the British, partly inspiring a mutiny in the Royal Indian Navy; unsatisfied with Cripps's plans and Congress's understanding of them, Jinnah holds a Muslim "Direct Action Day" in August; riots connected to the Direct Action Day result in 5,000 deaths in Calcutta; Gandhi travels to Bengal to try to halt communal violence there.

1947 Louis Mountbatten replaces Archibald Wavell as viceroy and grows convinced that only partition will prevent large-scale violence in India; Nehru and

1965
India and Pakistan fight their second war over Kashmir

1971
East Pakistan becomes independent Bangladesh

1992
The Babri Masjid riots revive Hindu-Muslim violence in India

1999
Pervez Musharraf stages a military coup and takes over Pakistan

1947 — **2003**

1947
India and Pakistan become independent as the subcontinent is partitioned

1984
Indian Prime Minister Indira Gandhi is assassinated by Sikh separatists

1998
India and Pakistan become official nuclear powers

2003
India and Pakistan begin talks on Kashmir

123

Jinnah agree on partition; Sir Cyril Radcliffe draws the borders separating India and Pakistan; both nations achieve independence in mid-August, as riots, murders, and mass migrations bring chaos to the Punjab; the status of Kashmir results in the first Indo-Pakistani war.

1948 Mahatma Gandhi is assassinated by Hindu fundamentalists; Muhammad Ali Jinnah dies.

1950 India's government ratifies its new constitution; Jinnah's successor, Liaquat Ali Khan, is assassinated.

1956 Prime Minister Nehru divides India's states along mostly linguistic lines.

1958 Mohammad Ayub Khan becomes military dictator of Pakistan.

1962 India and China fight an indecisive war over disputed border regions.

1964 Jawaharlal Nehru dies.

1965 Nehru's daughter, Indira Gandhi, becomes prime minister; the second Indo-Pakistani war is fought over border disputes, including those in Kashmir; East Pakistani leader Sheikh Mujibur Rahman proposes greater autonomy for East Pakistan.

1971 The third Indo-Pakistani war is fought over the status of East Pakistan; East Pakistan gains its independence as Bangladesh; Pakistan's second military dictator, Aga Muhammad Yahya Khan, surrenders authority to politician Zulfikar Ali Bhutto; Indira Gandhi abolishes the last of the official privileges held by India's hereditary princes.

1972 Agreements establish a semi-official "line of control" dividing Kashmir.

1974 India stages its first nuclear tests.

1975 Indira Gandhi declares an "emergency," limiting civil rights.

1977 The "emergency" is lifted; Ali Bhutto is ousted in favor of General Muhammad Zia ul-Haq.

1979 Ali Bhutto is executed after being found guilty of participation in a political murder.

1984 The Indian Army tries to suppress Sikh separatists in the Punjab; Indira Gandhi is assassinated; Rajiv Gandhi, her son, becomes prime minister.

1988 General Zia ul-Haq dies in an airplane crash; Benazir Bhutto, Ali's daughter, becomes Pakistan's leader.

1991 Rajiv Gandhi is assassinated by Tamil separatists based in Sri Lanka; Nawaz Sharif replaces Benazir Bhutto.

1992 The Babri Masjid riots take place between Hindus and Muslims across India; the Indian government lifts many of Nehru's socialist-oriented economic restrictions.

1993 Benazir Bhutto is elected to replace Nawaz Sharif.

1997 New elections in Pakistan return Sharif to office.

1998 Both India and Pakistan become official nuclear powers; Sonia Gandhi, Rajiv's wife, becomes president of the Congress-I party.

1999 Pervez Musharraf stages a military coup, replacing Nawaz Sharif; India's population passes one billion.

2003 Musharraf and Indian Prime Minister Atal Behari Vajpayee open up talks on Kashmir.

2004 Elections return the Congress-I party to power in India, but Sonia Gandhi refuses to serve as prime minister.

2005 India and Pakistan discuss turning the Kashmiri Line of Control into a "soft border"; movement across it as well as across the borders in the Punjab and Sind is eased.

Chapter 1

1. Quoted in Tariq Ali, "Bitter Chill of Winter," *London Review of Books*, XXIII, 8 (April 19, 2001), pp. 43–48.
2. Anthony Read and David Fisher, *The Proudest Day: India's Long Road to Independence*. London: Jonathan Cape, 1997, p. 503.
3. Trevor Royle, *The Last Days of the Raj*. London: Michael Joseph, 1989, pp. 192–195.

Chapter 2

4. Fritz Blackwell, *India: A Global Studies Handbook*. Santa Barbara, CA: ABC-Clio, 2004, p. 210.
5. Stanley Wolpert, *A New History of India*, 5th ed. New York: Oxford University Press, 1997, p. 127.
6. Bamber Gascoigne, *The Great Moguls*. New York: Carroll and Graf Publishers, 2002, p. 69.

Chapter 3

7. Royle, *The Last Days of the Raj*, p. 3.
8. Percival Spear, *A History of India*, Vol. 2. Middlesex, UK: Penguin Books, 1965, p. 85.
9. Quoted in Geoffrey Moorhouse, *Calcutta*. New York: Holt, Rinehart, and Winston, 1973, p. 59.
10. Ibid., p. 219.
11. Wolpert, *A New History of India*, p. 240.
12. Royle, *The Last Days of the Raj*, pp. 153–154.
13. Shahid Javed Burki, *Pakistan: Fifty Years of Nationhood*, 3rd ed. Boulder, CO: Westview Press, 1999, p. 3.
14. Wolpert, *A New History of India*, p. 290.
15. Quoted in Lawrence James, *The Rise and Fall of the British Empire*. London: Abacus, 1995, p. 418.
16. Read and Fisher, *The Proudest Day*, p. 9.
17. Wolpert, *A New History of India*, p. 300.

Chapter 4

18. Read and Fisher, *The Proudest Day*, pp. 71–76.
19. Quoted in Ibid., p. 81.
20. Wolpert, *A New History of India*, pp. 273–275.
21. Read and Fisher, *The Proudest Day*, pp. 90–93.
22. Ibid., pp. 107–108.
23. Ved Mehta, *Mahatma Gandhi and His Apostles*. Middlesex, UK: Penguin Books, 1976, pp. 142–144.
24. Read and Fisher, *The Proudest Day*, pp. 227–230.
25. Quoted in Ibid., p. 225.
26. Jan Morris, *Farewell the Trumpets: An Imperial Retreat*. London: Penguin Books, 1979, p. 286.
27. Quoted in Ibid., p. 293.
28. Royle, *The Last Days of the Raj*, p. 56.
29. Wolpert, *A New History of India*, p. 233.
30. Ibid. pp. 324–326.
31. Spear, *A History of India*, p. 218.
32. Quoted in Royle, *The Last Days of the Raj*, p. 84.
33. Dominique LaPierre and Larry Collins, *Freedom at Midnight*. New Delhi: Vikas Publishing House, 1997.
34. Wolpert, *A New History of India*, p. 336.
35. Ibid. p. 333.

Chapter 5

36. Quoted in Read and Fisher, *The Proudest Day*, p. 234.
37. LaPierre and Collins, *Freedom at Midnight*, p. 33.
38. Ibid., p. 127.
39. Wolpert, *A New History of India*, p. 323.
40. Ibid., p. 325.
41. Quoted in Ibid., p. 330.
42. Read and Fisher, *The Proudest Day*, p. 296.
43. Ibid., p. 358.
44. James, *The Rise and Fall of the British Empire*, p. 549.
45. Quoted in LaPierre and Collins, *Freedom at Midnight*, p. 133.
46. Burki, *Pakistan*, p. 7.
47. Read and Fisher, *The Proudest Day*, p. 389.
48. Ibid., p. 390.
49. Wolpert, *A New History of India*, p. 344.
50. Morris., *Farewell the Trumpets*, p. 483.
51. Quoted in Read and Fisher, *The Proudest Day*, p. 398.
52. Ibid., p. 400.
53. Quoted in Wolpert, *A New History of India*, p. 345.
54. Spear, *A History of India*, p. 236.
55. Morris, *Farewell the Trumpets*, p. 486.

Chapter 6

56. LaPierre and Collins, *Freedom at Midnight*, pp. 36–40.
57. Quoted in Read and Fisher, *The Proudest Day*, p. 443.
58. Ibid., p. 438.
59. Ibid., p. 501.
60. LaPierre and Collins, *Freedom at Midnight*, p. 203.
61. Quoted in Read and Fisher, *The Proudest Day*, p. 467.
62. Ibid., p. 468.
63. Wolpert, *A New History of India*, p. 348.
64. LaPierre and Collins, *Freedom at Midnight*, pp. 226–228.
65. Ibid., p. 287.
66. Read and Fisher, *The Proudest Day*, pp. 484–495.
67. LaPierre and Collins, *Freedom at Midnight*, pp. 298–301.
68. Quoted in Read and Fisher, *The Proudest Day*, p. 491.
69. Quoted in Wolpert, *A New History of India*, p. 349.
70. Royle, *The Last Days of the Raj*, p. 180.
71. Quoted in Read and Fisher, *The Proudest Day*, p. 495.
72. Burki, *Pakistan*, p. 25.
73. Quoted in LaPierre and Collins, *Freedom at Midnight*, p. 321.

Chapter 7

74. Quoted in LaPierre and Collins, *Freedom at Midnight*, p. 362.
75. Shashi Tharoor, *India: From Midnight to the Millennium*. New York: HarperPerennial, 1998, pp. 14–15.
76. Barbara D. Metcalf and Thomas R. Metcalf, *A Concise History of India*. Cambridge, UK: Cambridge University Press, 2002, p. 217.
77. Read and Fisher, *The Proudest Day*, pp. 393–397.
78. Ibid., p. 400.
79. Ibid., p. 403.
80. Wolpert, *A New History of India*, pp. 346–347.
81. Read and Fisher, *The Proudest Day*, p. 404.
82. Quoted in Wolpert, *A New History of India*, p. 347.
83. Mehta, *Mahatma Gandhi*, pp. 184–190.
84. Wolpert, *A New History of India*, p. 346.
85. LaPierre and Collins, *Freedom at Midnight*, p. 101.
86. Royle, *The Last Days of the Raj*, p. 180.
87. Quoted in Ibid., p. 196.
88. Read and Fisher, *The Proudest Day*, p. 492.
89. Quoted in LaPierre and Collins, *Freedom at Midnight*, p. 309.
90. Quoted in James, *The Rise and Fall of the British Empire*, p. 554.
91. LaPierre and Collins, p. 402.
92. Ibid., p. 378.
93. Quoted in Mark Tully and Zareer Masani, *From Raj to Rajiv*. London: BBC Books, 1998, p. 17.
94. Quoted in Morris, *Farewell the Trumpets*, p. 493.
95. Tully and Masani, *From Raj to Rajiv*, p. 20.

Chapter 8

96. Quoted in Wolpert, *A New History of India*, p. 441.
97. Ibid., p. 352.
98. Blackwell, *India*, pp. 80–81.
99. Ibid., p. 83.
100. Metcalf and Metcalf, *A Concise History of India*, p. 236.
101. Tully and Masani, *From Raj to Rajiv*, pp. 146–147.
102. Metcalf and Metcalf, *A Concise History of India*, p. 252.
103. Ibid., p. 258.
104. Blackwell, *India*, pp. 44–45.
105. Tully and Masani, *From Raj to Rajiv*, p. 82.
106. Tharoor, *India*, p. 77.
107. Metcalf and Metcalf, *A Concise History of India*, pp. 269–270.
108. Wolpert, *A New History of India*, p. 444.
109. Metcalf and Metcalf, *A Concise History of India*, p. 279.
110. Ibid., pp. 238–242.
111. Ibid., p. 284.
112. Wolpert, *A New History of India*, p. 432.
113. Tharoor, *India*, p. 349.

Chapter 9

114. Wolpert, *A New History of India*, p. 373.
115. Salman Rushdie, *Shame*. London: Jonathan Cape, 1983, p. 83.
116. Wolpert, *A New History of India*, p. 387.
117. Robert LaPorte, Jr., "Pakistan: A Nation

Still in the Making," in Selig S. Harrison, Paul H. Kreisberg, and Dennis Kux, eds., *India and Pakistan: The First Fifty Years.* Cambridge, UK: Cambridge University Press, 1999, p. 48.

118. Burki, *Pakistan*, p. 48.

119. Quoted in Read and Fisher, *The Proudest Day*, p. 491.

120. Bennet Jones, *Pakistan: Eye of the Storm.* New Haven, CT: Yale University Press, 2002, pp. 228–229.

121. Burki, *Pakistan*, p. 52.

122. Ibid., pp. 219–220.

123. Anita M. Weiss, "Pakistan: Some Progress, Sobering Challenges," in Selig, et al., *India and Pakistan*, pp. 142–143.

124. Wolpert, *A New History of India*, p. 452.

125. LaPorte, in Selig, et al., *India and Pakistan*, pp. 58–59.

126. Burki, *Pakistan*, p. 119.

127. Ibid., p. 139.

128. Marvin G. Weinbaum, "Pakistan: Misplaced Priorities, Missed Opportunities," in Selig et al., *India and Pakistan*, p. 96.

Ali, Tariq. *The Nehrus and the Gandhis: An Indian Dynasty.* London: Picador, 1985.

Azad, Maulana Abdul Kalam. *India Wins Freedom: An Autobiographical Narrative.* New York: Longman's, Green, 1960.

Blackwell, Fritz. *India: A Global Studies Handbook.* Santa Barbara, CA: ABC-Clio, 2004.

Burki, Shaheed Javed. *Pakistan: Fifty Years of Nationhood,* 3rd ed. Boulder, CO: Westview Press, 1999.

Das, Gurcharan. *India Unbound.* New York: Anchor Books, 2001.

Edwardes, Michael. *The Myth of the Mahatma: Gandhi, the British, and the Raj.* London: Constable: 1988.

Gascoigne, Bamber. *A Brief History of the Great Moguls.* New York: Carroll and Graf, 2002.

Ghose, Sankar. *Modern Indian Political Thought.* New Delhi: Allied Ltd., 1984.

Griffith, Kenneth. *The Discovery of Nehru: An Experience of India.* London: Michael Joseph, 1989.

Hansen, Waldemar. *The Peacock Throne.* New York: Holt, Rinehart, and Winston, 1972.

Harrison, Selig S., Paul H. Kreisberg, and Dennis Kux, eds. *India and Pakistan: The First Fifty Years.* Cambridge, UK: Cambridge University Press, 1999.

Hay, Jeff, ed. *Europe Rules the World, 1848–1913.* San Diego, CA: Greenhaven Press, 2001.

Hibbert, Christopher. *The Great Mutiny: India 1857.* Middlesex, UK: Penguin Books, 1980.

James, Lawrence. *The Rise and Fall of the British Empire.* London: Abacus, 1998.

Jones, Bennett. *Pakistan: Eye of the Storm.* New Haven, CT: Yale University Press, 2002.

Keay, John. *India: A History.* New York: Atlantic-Grove, 2001.

LaPierre, Dominique, and Larry Collins. *Freedom at Midnight,* new ed. New Delhi: Vikas, 1997.

Low, D. A. *Britain and Indian Nationalism, 1929–1942.* Cambridge, UK: Cambridge University Press, 1997.

Mahmud, S. F. *A Concise History of Indo-Pakistan.* Karachi: Oxford University Press, 1988.

Mehta, Ved. *A Family Affair: India Under Three Prime Ministers.* New York: Oxford University Press, 1982.

——. *Mahatma Ghandi and His Apostles.* Middlesex, UK: Penguin, 1977.

Metcalf, Barbara D., and Thomas R. Metcalf. *A Concise History of India.* Cambridge, UK: Cambridge University Press, 2002.

Moorhouse, Geoffrey. *Calcutta.* New York: Holt, Rinehart, and Winston, 1973.

——. *India Britannica: A Vivid Introduction to the History of British India.* New York: Harper and Row, 1983.

Morris, Jan. *Farewell the Trumpets: An Imperial Retreat.* London: Penguin, 1978.

——. *Heaven's Command: An Imperial Progress.* London: Penguin, 1973.

Mukherjee, Aditya, and Mridula Mukherjee. *India After Independence.* Middlesex, UK: Viking Penguin, 1999.

Pandey, Gyanendra. *Remembering Partition: Violence, Nationalism, and History in India.* Cambridge, UK: Cambridge University Press, 2001.

Read, Anthony, and David Fisher. *The Proudest Day: India's Long Road to Independence.* London: Jonathan Cape, 1997.

Royle, Trevor. *The Last Days of the Raj.* London: Michael Joseph, 1989.

Sarkar, Sumit. *Modern India 1885–1947*. London: Macmillan, 1989.

Singh, Khushwant. *Train to Pakistan*. New York: Grove Press, 1956.

Sofri, Gianni. *Gandhi and India*, trans. Janet Sethre. New York: Interlink, 1999.

Spear, Percival. *A History of India*, Vol. 2. Middlesex, UK: Penguin, 1965.

Talbot, Ian. *India and Pakistan*. New York: Arnold and Oxford University Press, 2000.

Tan, Tai Yong, and Gyanesh Kudaisya. *The Aftermath of Partition in South Asia*. London: Routledge, 2000.

Thapar, Romila. *A History of India*, Vol. 1. Middlesex, UK: Penguin Books, 1966.

Tharoor, Shashi. *India: From Midnight to the Millennium*. New York: HarperPerennial, 1998.

Tully, Mark, and Zareer Masani. *From Raj to Rajiv*. London: BBC Books, 1988.

Van der Veer, Peter. *Religious Nationalism: Hindus and Muslims in India*. Berkeley, CA: University of California Press, 1994.

Wolpert, Stanley. *Gandhi's Passion: The Life and Legacy of Mahatma Gandhi*. New York: Oxford University Press, 2002.

———. *Jinnah of Pakistan*. New York: Oxford University Press, 1985.

———. *A New History of India*, 5th ed. New York: Oxford University Press, 1997.

page:

Jeff Hay is a lecturer in History at San Diego State University. A specialist in twentieth-century world history, he is the author of the four-volume *History of the Third Reich*, which was recognized by the American Library Association as an outstanding reference work of 2003. He is also the author of *An Encyclopedia of the Vietnam War* and the editor of numerous anthologies, including *The Treaty of Versailles* and *Living Through the End of the Cold War*.

George J. Mitchell served as chairman of the peace negotiations in Northern Ireland during the 1990s. Under his leadership, a historic accord, ending decades of conflict, was agreed to by the governments of Ireland and the United Kingdom and the political parties in Northern Ireland. In May 1998, the agreement was overwhelmingly endorsed by a referendum of the voters of Ireland, North and South. Senator Mitchell's leadership earned him worldwide praise and a Nobel Peace Prize nomination. He accepted his appointment to the U.S. Senate in 1980. After leaving the Senate, Senator Mitchell joined the Washington, D.C. law firm of Piper Rudnick, where he now practices law. Senator Mitchell's life and career have embodied a deep commitment to public service and he continues to be active in worldwide peace and disarmament efforts.

James I. Matray is Professor of History and Chair at California State University, Chico. He has published more than forty articles and book chapters on U.S.–Korean relations during and after World War II. Author of *The Reluctant Crusade: American Foreign Policy in Korea, 1941–1950* and *Japan's Emergence as a Global Power*, his most recent publication is *East Asia and the United States: An Encyclopledia of Relations Since 1784*. Matray also is international columnist for the *Donga Ilbo* in South Korea.